T0162610

THE
Sentimental
KITCHEN

delicious dishes from family and friends

JANET L. GAEBEL

Inspiring Voices®
A Service of **Guideposts**

Inspiring Voices books may be ordered through booksellers or by contacting:

Inspiring Voices
1663 Liberty Drive
Bloomington, IN 47403
www.inspiringvoices.com
1 (866) 697-5313

Because of the dynamic nature of the Internet, any web addresses or links contained in this book may have changed since publication and may no longer be valid. The views expressed in this work are solely those of the author and do not necessarily reflect the views of the publisher, and the publisher hereby disclaims any responsibility for them.

Any people depicted in stock imagery provided by Thinkstock are models, and such images are being used for illustrative purposes only. Certain stock imagery © Thinkstock.

ISBN: 978-1-4624-0829-0 (sc)
ISBN: 978-1-4624-0830-6 (e)

Library of Congress Control Number: 2013921049

Printed in the United States of America.

Inspiring Voices rev. date: 11/19/2013

CONTENTS

1. **Appetizers** 1
   Beanless Bean Dip 3
   Buffalo Wings. 4
   Curt's Stuffed Mushrooms 5
   Delicious Fruit Dip. 6
   Dill Dip 7
   Mama's Fresh Garden Salsa. 8
   Mama's Great Guacamole. 9
   Pâté. 10
   Spinach Dip 11
   Zesty Cocktail Sauce (for Shrimp Cocktail) 12

2. **Beverages**. 13
   Bloody Mary. 15
   Creamy Hot Cocoa. 16
   Holiday Eggnog 17
   Homemade Kahlua. 18
   Hot Apple Cider 19
   Long Island Iced Tea. 20
   Margarita Recipe 21
   Party Sangria 22

3. **Breads** 23
   Beginner's Basic Sourdough Starter. .25
   Blueberry Surprise Muffins 26
   Butter Crescents 27
   Cherry Breakfast Scones 28
   Cinnabon Clone 29
   Cream Cheese Banana Bread 30
   Holiday Cranberry Nut Bread. 31
   Pumpernickel Rye Bread. 32
   Cheddar Bay Biscuits Copycat 33
   Spicy Cornbread 34
   Sprouted Whole Wheat Health Bread. 35
   Zucchini Bread. 36

4. **Breakfast** 37
   Breakfast Crepes with Berries 39
   Easy Overnight Caramel Pecan Rolls .40

Eggs Benedict 41
German Apple Pancake 42
Healthy Swiss Muesli 43
Mama's Buckwheat Pancakes 44
Omelet Supreme 45
Sour Cream Coffee Cake 46
Sourdough Pancakes 47
Strawberry–Cream Cheese Stuffed French Toast 48

5. Main Dishes 49
Barbecue Brisket 51
Beef and Noodles 52
Beef Rouladen 53
Beef Wellington 54
Daddy's Corned Beef and Cabbage 55
Goulash 56
Mama's Beef Stroganoff 57
Pioneer Woman's Prime Rib with Rosemary Salt Crust 58
Simple Simon Salmon 59
Sweet Baby Salmon 60
Sweet Orange Tilapia 61
Yum Yums 62

6. Salads 63
Apple Jicama Coleslaw 65
Sugar-Free Cranberry Relish 66
Crispy Garlic Parmesan Croutons 67
Curt's Fruit Salad 68
Greek Vinaigrette Salad Dressing 69
Hot German Potato Salad 70
Mama's Garlic House Dressing 71
Ramen Broccoli Cole Slaw (Wedding Salad) 72
Blue Cheese Dressing 73
Seafood Pasta Salad 74
Strawberry Pretzel Salad 75
Taco Salad 76
Thousand Island Dressing 77

7. Side Dishes 79
Calico Baked Beans 81
Cauliflower Mac-and-Cheese Casserole 82
Classic Creamed Spinach 83
Corn and Oyster Casserole 84

Creamed Corn Like No Other 85
Delicious Dill Potato Salad. 86
Hash Brown Casserole 87
Mama's Sweet Potato Soufflé. 88
Restaurant-Style Fried Rice. 89
Twice Baked Potatoes 90

8. **Soups and Stews** 91
Beef Barley Soup. 93
Chicken Tortilla Soup. 94
Daddy's Oyster Soup 95
Egg Drop Soup. 96
Ham and Bean Soup. 97
Loaded Baked Potato Soup 98
Mama's Lentil Chili 99
Seafood Gumbo 100
Split Pea and Ham Soup. 101
Yummy Minestrone 102

9. **Sweets and Desserts** 103
Aunt Vicki's Melt-in-Your-Mouth Dessert. 105
Chewy Pumpkin Bars. 106
Chocolate and Almond Biscotti 107
Coconut Lime Bars. 108
Daddy's Homemade Ice Cream. 109
Grandma Joyce's Oven Caramel Corn 110
Grandma Wilson's Red Velvet Cake 111
Krispy Caramel Bars. 112
Mama's Best Chocolate Chip Cookies 113
Mama's Flaky Pie Crust 114
Mango Ice Cream. 115
Rustic Apple Tart 116
Sinful Pumpkin Bars 117

Glossary. 119
Glossary of Cooking Terminology 121

FOREWORD

Dear Daughter,

Inside, you will find a collection of recipes that I have gathered and created over the years since you were born. I now share these recipes with you, my dear Lindsey, for you to share with your children, friends, family, and generations to come. I was inspired to do this because of all the times you've called to ask me for the recipe for one of the dishes that I prepared for you while you were growing up.

I have worked many days and nights to collect these recipes from friends and family members alike, so that you can have this collection at your fingertips all in one volume. They are the creations of those who love you every bit as much as I love you. Every ingredient has been tried and tested to produce only the best results. You will remember having eaten just about every dish inside this cookbook. It is not only a cookbook but also a memory book.

Each recipe includes a short story to help jog your memory a bit. Writing this book brought back a lot of fond memories of Grandma Nell, Grandpa Frank, Grandpa Rich, and you, especially from when you were growing up. You were very inquisitive as a child and so full of love for different foods. It also has recipes from Daddy, Curt, Grandma Gaebel, and others who love you.

Your diagnosis of Type I Diabetes at age two, my darling Lindsey, didn't hinder you from trying new foods. It only forced me to be more creative in how I made dishes for you, so they were a little healthier and more diabetic-friendly. That's not to say that this is a diabetic cookbook. You, as any child, were hungry for new dishes. Yet you were open to try the unusual, so I tried new and different foods. You gobbled them up, and I thank you for that, my love.

On the top of each page, I included an aphorism or Bible verse that I thought was special. I thought you could take these quotes to heart, and I hope you like what you read. They really hit home to me, and I felt they might touch your heart as well.

Anyway, sweetheart, here is your cookbook for you to take and use in your own kitchen for your own family and friends; take it and use it with love and happiness. Make notes in it and make changes in it as you see fit to make the recipes truly your own. I love you, and I hope you enjoy it.

I've written this cookbook for my daughter and anyone else who can benefit from good, home cooked dishes. I've included sentiments with each recipe which I hope can touch your hearts as they have mine. Enjoy this book not so much as a cookbook but as a guidebook that you can keep close to your heart. I hope you enjoy using it as much as I did writing it. With love and adornment,

Janet Gaebel

November, 2013

"I will keep telling you that you are important, deserving, loving, intelligent, worthy, compassionate, beautiful, creative, inspiring, brave, true, strong, and able until you finally realize it for yourself."

—Author Unknown

1. APPETIZERS

BEANLESS BEAN DIP

I made this every time your dad had his friends and family over for football parties. It's easy to throw together, and it's a winner at any party. Just throw everything into the slow cooker and serve with tortilla chips. Keep this one where you'll be sure to find it.

> "Eat diamonds for breakfast and shine all day."
> —Unknown

1 15-oz. can chili with no beans
1 lb. hamburger

1 lb. Velveeta cheese, cubed

Procedure

1. Place all ingredients in slow cooker. Cook on high until hamburger is cooked through, about 3 to 4 hours. Reduce setting to low until ready to serve, stirring occasionally.
2. Serve with tortilla chips.

Yield: 24 servings
Degree of Difficulty: Easy
Preparation Time: 15 minutes
Cooking Time: 4 hour and 30 minutes
Total Time: 4 hour and 45 minutes

Recipe Type

Appetizer

BUFFALO WINGS

This recipe is great for football or other parties. It makes about twenty-four wings. It tastes good and is easy to make. Line your broiler pan with foil, and it's easy to clean up. I included a recipe for blue cheese dip, so you're set, baby-doll!

> "Far away in the sunshine are my highest aspirations. I may not reach them, but I can look up and see the beauty, believe in them and try to follow where they lead."
> —Louisa May Alcott

2 lb. chicken wings (about 24 wings)
3 Tbs. butter, melted
6 Tbs. bottled hot pepper sauce
2 Tbs. paprika
1/2 tsp. salt
1 Tbs. cayenne pepper
1/4 tsp. black pepper
celery sticks (optional)

Blue Cheese Dip
1/2 c. sour cream
1/2 c. crumbled blue cheese
1/2 c. mayonnaise
1 1/2 Tbs. white wine vinegar or white vinegar
2 cloves garlic, minced

Procedure

1. Cut off wing tips and discard or reserve for other use, such as making stock. Cut wings apart at the joint. Put chicken wing pieces in a plastic bag. Set aside. Food safety note: When cutting raw chicken, it is best to use a cutting board just for this purpose. Wash cutting board thoroughly when finished, and do not let raw chicken juices come in contact with other food.

2. Create a marinade by stirring together the melted butter, hot pepper sauce, paprika, salt, cayenne pepper, and black pepper. Pour all but 2 tablespoons of the marinade over the chicken pieces in the plastic bag. (Reserve remaining marinade for when the wings come out of the oven.) Seal bag and marinate at room temperature for half an hour.

3. Place wing pieces on a foil-lined broiler pan rack. Broil 4 to 5 inches from the heat for about 10 minutes on each side, until chicken is tender and no longer pink. Remove from oven and baste with reserved marinade. Serve with blue cheese dip and celery sticks if desired.

4. Blue cheese dip: Combine sour cream, mayonnaise, blue cheese, vinegar, and garlic in a blender or food processor. Blend or pulse until smooth. Cover and chill; good for up to a week.

Yield: 12 Servings
Degree of Difficulty: Easy
Preparation Time: 15 minutes
Cooking Time: 20 minutes
Total Time: 35 minutes

Recipe Type

Appetizer

CURT'S STUFFED MUSHROOMS

Curt served these stuffed mushrooms as appetizers at Thanksgiving, 2012. They are easy to prepare, and they are delicious. Maybe you can make them a part of your traditional family Thanksgiving.

"When you meet your Love, you invest your Life."

—Unknown

24 large button mushrooms, stems removed
2 (8-oz.) packages cream cheese, softened

4 strips bacon, cooked crispy
3 Tbs. chives

Procedure

1. Turn oven on to broil.
2. Clean mushrooms. Combine cream cheese with crumbled bacon and chives. Place spoonful of mixture into each mushroom and set on cookie sheet.
3. Broil until cream cheese bubbles and begins to brown, about 3 to 5 minutes.
4. Serve hot.

Yield: 24 Servings
Degree of Difficulty: Easy
Preparation Time: 20 minutes
Cooking Time: 5 minutes
Total Time: 25 minutes

Recipe Type

Appetizer

DELICIOUS FRUIT DIP

I got this recipe from a Tupperware party years ago, and it's as good today as it was then. I serve it with apples, oranges, and pineapple, and it's delicious!

"Watch, stand fast in the faith, be brave, be strong. Let all that you do be done with love."

—1 Corinthians 16:13 NKJV

1 (3.5 oz.) pkg. vanilla instant pudding mix
c. sour cream

1 c. orange juice concentrate

Procedure

1. Stir all ingredients together and serve with desired type of fruit.

Yield: 10 Servings
Degree of Difficulty: Very Easy

Preparation Time: 10 minutes
Total Time: 10 minutes

Recipe Type

Appetizer

DILL DIP

This is another dip recipe that I would often serve at family parties or potlucks. Like the spinach dip, you can make this fat-free by using fat-free varieties of mayo and sour cream.

> "One day in retrospect the years of struggle will strike you as the most beautiful."
> —Sigmund Freud

1 tsp. dill weed
1 tsp. Beau Monde seasoning
1 tsp. parsley flakes

1 tsp. onion flakes
1 c. sour cream
1 c. mayonnaise

Procedure

1. Combine all ingredients; mix well. Refrigerate at least 2 hours in a covered container. Serve with fresh vegetables.

Yield: 24 servings
Degree of Difficulty: Easy
Preparation Time: 10 minutes

Inactive Time: 2 hours
Total Time: 2 hours and 10 minutes

Recipe Type

Appetizer

MAMA'S FRESH GARDEN SALSA

This is the salsa recipe I make when I can get the freshest ingredients, usually in the summertime. It's simple to throw everything in the food processor and whip up the salsa in a jiffy. I like to serve it with fresh, home-baked tortilla chips, but bagged chips work well too. This is a spicy recipe, so you can tone it down if you wish by cutting down the amount of jalapeños or by removing the seeds. I personally like to leave the seeds in, because I prefer it spicy.

"There is no greatness where there is no simplicity, goodness and truth."

—Leo Tolstoy

1 medium red onion, quartered
3 cloves garlic
2 jalapeño peppers, halved
3 large tomatoes, quartered

1/3 bunch cilantro
1 lime, juiced
salt and pepper to taste

Procedure

1. In large food processor, add red onion, garlic cloves, and jalapeño peppers. Pulse until vegetables are chopped into medium pieces. Add cilantro and pulse until chopped.
2. Add tomatoes, lime juice, and salt and pepper; pulse until chopped but not pulverized. Transfer to serving bowl. Serve with tortilla chips.

Yield: 12 servings
Degree of Difficulty: Easy
Preparation Time: 15 minutes
Total Time: 15 minutes

Recipe Type

Appetizer

MAMA'S GREAT GUACAMOLE

I don't think your cookbook would be complete without a recipe for guacamole. It's simple to throw together and tastes delicious. Don't forget to save the pits to grow an avocado plant.

"He liked to like people, therefore people liked him."
—Mark Twain

2 medium avocados, peeled, pitted, and diced
4 cloves garlic, minced
1 fresh jalapeño pepper, seeded and chopped
1/2 medium tomato, chopped

2 Tbs. onion, finely chopped
kosher salt to taste
2 tsp. fresh lime juice
3 Tbs. cilantro

Procedure

1. Cut avocado in half and remove pit. Score each half and spoon fruit into bowl. In food processor, add garlic, jalapeño, onion, and cilantro. Pulse until chopped finely. Divide tomato in half and add to food processor. Pulse until tomato is chopped into small chunks but not pulverized. Salt to taste and stir together. Sprinkle with lime juice and cilantro and then stir and taste again. Add more garlic, jalapeño.
2. Add tomato mixture to avocado and add salt, lime juice, and cilantro as desired. Stir to combine, being careful not to break up avocado too much. Serve with tortilla chips.

Yield: 8 Servings (2 cups)
Degree of Difficulty: Easy
Preparation Time: 15 minutes
Inactive Time: 2 hours
Total Time: 2 hours and 15 minutes

Recipe Type

Appetizer

PÂTÉ

This is the recipe for the pâté that I made for every New Year's Eve we celebrated at home. It's really called Poor Man's Pâté because it doesn't use really expensive ingredients. But it is good and always goes over well at parties. Its few ingredients make it simple to prepare. It has cream cheese in it, so it's no surprise that you like it.

"Love yourself, appreciate yourself, see the good in you ... and respect yourself."
—Betty Shabazz, Educator

1 (8-oz.) package cream cheese
1 (8-oz.) package braunschweiger (liver sausage)
1 tsp. grated onion
2 tsp. lemon juice

1 tsp. Worcestershire sauce
salt and pepper to taste
parsley flakes (optional)

Procedure

1. Mash and blend cream cheese and braunschweiger until combined well. Blend in remaining ingredients except for the parsley flakes.
2. Form into a ball and roll in parsley flakes if desired.
3. Best if chilled overnight.

Yield: 20 Servings
Degree of Difficulty: Easy
Preparation Time: 15 minutes
Total Time: 15 minutes

Recipe Type

Appetizer

SPINACH DIP

This is a simple veggie dip to throw together for a party or potluck. You do need to plan ahead, as it needs to marinate a bit to taste its best. If you use fat-free sour cream and mayo, it's a healthy dip you can enjoy without any guilt.

> "Don't let yesterday use too much of today."
> —Will Rogers

1 c. sour cream
1 c. mayonnaise
2 cloves garlic, minced
1 c. onion, finely chopped

1 (8-oz.) can water chestnuts, chopped
1 (10-oz.) package frozen leaf spinach,
   thawed and squeezed dry
1 packet vegetable soup mix

Procedure

1. Mix all ingredients together and refrigerate for at least 3 hours. Serve with fresh vegetables.

Yield: 15 Servings
Degree of Difficulty: Easy

Preparation Time: 10 minutes
Inactive Time: 3 hours
Total Time: 3 hours and 10 minutes

Recipe Type

Appetizer

ZESTY COCKTAIL SAUCE (FOR SHRIMP COCKTAIL)

This the recipe Daddy uses for his famous shrimp cocktail. It's simple and gets better as it sits. Here's to Daddy!

> "No regrets, just good times, love, peace, and lots of chocolates."
>
> —Unknown

1 c. catsup
2 Tbs. prepared ground horseradish
1 Tbs. Worcestershire sauce

1 tsp. lemon juice
Dash garlic powder

Procedure

1. Mix all ingredients together and refrigerate until ready to serve with cleaned shrimp.

Yield: 12 Servings
Preparation Time: 5 minutes
Inactive Time: 1 hour
Total Time: 1 hour and 5 minutes

Recipe Type

Appetizer

2. BEVERAGES

BLOODY MARY

No cookbook would be complete without a recipe for bloody mary mix. This is a staple in any bar, and most people love this cocktail, so you will need to keep it on hand.

"Prayer unfolds in the stillness of the soul."
—Unknown

8 oz. vegetable juice cocktail
1 oz. vodka
1 tsp. lemon juice
1 Tbs. Worcestershire sauce
1 tsp. prepared horseradish
2 tsp. hot pepper sauce

Salt and black pepper to taste
Dash celery salt
1 celery stalk
1 large green olive
1 dill pickle spear

Procedure

1. Fill tall glass with ice and 1 shot of vodka, vegetable juice, lemon juice, Worcestershire sauce, horseradish, and hot pepper sauce. Add dash celery salt and salt and pepper to taste. Garnish with celery stick, green olives, and dill pickle.

Yield: 1 Serving
Degree of Difficulty: Very Easy
Preparation Time: 10 minutes
Total Time: 10 minutes

Recipe Type

Beverage

CREAMY HOT COCOA

There's nothing more soothing than a cup of Creamy Hot Cocoa on a cold winter's day. Homemade cocoa isn't difficult, and it's well worth the small effort. Next time you're in the mood to snuggle up with a good book and a cup of hot cocoa, try this recipe. It's the best one I know.

> "The time is always right to do what is right."
>
> —Martin Luther King Jr.

1/3 c. unsweetened cocoa powder
3/4 c. granulated sugar
1 pinch salt
1/2 c. boiling water

3 3/4 c. milk
1 tsp. vanilla extract
3/4 c. half-and-half

Procedure

1. Combine the cocoa, sugar, and pinch of salt in a saucepan. Blend in the boiling water. Bring this mixture to an easy boil while you stir. Simmer and stir for about 2 minutes. Watch that it doesn't scorch. Stir in milk and heat until very hot, but do not boil. Remove from heat and add vanilla. Divide between 4 mugs. Add the half-and-half to the filled mugs to cool cocoa to drinking temperature.

Yield: 4 Servings
Degree of Difficulty: Easy

Recipe Type

Beverage

HOLIDAY EGGNOG

Do you remember the Christmas that we made homemade eggnog? It was rich and creamy, the best I've ever tasted! You had to prod me, but it was well worth it. The recipe made so much, though, that we had to throw some out; what a shame! When you make this eggnog, be sure to have enough people around to finish it before it spoils.

"Happiness is an exercise in endurance."
—Unknown

6 large eggs plus 2 yolks
1/2 c. granulated sugar
1/2 tsp. salt
4 c. whole milk
1/2 c. brandy, bourbon, or dark rum

1 1/2 Tbs. vanilla extract
1/2 tsp. grated nutmeg
1/4 c. heavy cream, whipped to soft peaks
Additional grated nutmeg for garnish

Procedure

1. Before heating, combine eggs, egg yolks, sugar, and salt in a heavy 3- or 4-quart pan, whisking until well-combined. Continue whisking while pouring milk into mixture in a slow, steady stream until completely incorporated.
2. Turn burner to lowest possible heat setting. Place pan on burner and stir continuously until an instant-read thermometer reaches 160 degrees F and the mixture thickens enough to coat the back of a spoon. This should take about 25 to 30 minutes.
3. Strain mixture through a fine sieve into a large bowl to remove any small bits of egg that were accidentally cooked. Add brandy, bourbon, or dark rum plus vanilla extract and nutmeg. Stir to combine.
4. Pour into a glass pitcher, decanter, or container and cover with a lid or plastic wrap. Refrigerate this custard mixture to chill at least 4 hours or up to 3 days before finishing eggnog.
5. When ready to serve, pour heavy cream into a bowl and whip until soft peaks form. Fold whipped cream into cold custard mixture until combined.
6. Serve in chilled glasses and garnish with a sprinkle of nutmeg.

Yield: 12 to 16 Servings
Degree of Difficulty: Easy
Preparation Time: 20 minutes
Total Time: 20 minutes

Recipe Type

Beverage

HOMEMADE KAHLUA

Here's a recipe for copycat Kahlua that you can make in your own kitchen. You need to plan ahead, since it ferments for a month, but it's worth it. This is a good one, sweetie pie!

"Help others achieve their dreams, and you will achieve yours."

—Les Brown

2 c. water
3 c. granulated sugar
1 whole vanilla bean, split in half
1/2 c. freeze-dried coffee

2 tsp. pure vanilla extract
1 (750-milliliter) bottle vodka
1 glass bottle with cap

Procedure

1. Boil the water and add sugar slowly. When the sugar is completely dissolved, add the coffee. Bring back to a boil for about 45 seconds. Stir in the vanilla extract.
2. Take the mixture off heat and let it cool to room temperature. Pour the vodka into the glass bottle. Cut the vanilla bean in half lengthwise and drop it into the bottle.
3. When the coffee mixture has cooled, add it to the glass bottle. Let sit in a cool, dry, dark place for one month. Enjoy!

Yield: 17 Servings
Degree of Difficulty: Easy
Preparation Time: 10 minutes
Total Time: 10 minutes

Recipe Type

Beverage

HOT APPLE CIDER

When you were very young and we still lived on the farm, Daddy and I sang in the church choir. This is a recipe for the Hot Apple Cider that we would drink after the choir went Christmas caroling together. It tasted pretty good and warmed us up as well. If I remember correctly, you came with us once or twice, as your Aunt Vicki and Joni each loved to have you at her side. If you make this cider, invite a crowd, as it makes a gallon. They will thank you for warming their hearts!

> "The future belongs to those who believe in the beauty of their dreams."
> —Eleanor Roosevelt

1 gallon apple cider or unfiltered apple juice
10 whole cloves
2 strips orange peel, about 2 in. long
8 Tbs. dried allspice

6 heads star anise
2 cinnamon sticks
1 (1-in.) piece fresh ginger, thinly sliced
Orange twists for garnish (optional)

Procedure

1. Combine all ingredients except the orange twists in a large pot. Bring the mixture to a boil over medium-high heat. Reduce heat to medium and simmer for 10 minutes.
2. Remove cider from heat and let steep for 10 minutes before serving. Serve the cider in heatproof mugs garnished with an orange twist, if desired.

Yield: 16
Degree of Difficulty: Easy
Preparation Time: 10 minutes

Recipe Type

Beverage

LONG ISLAND ICED TEA

I know how you like your iced tea, baby, so I thought I would include an alcoholic version just in case you want to take it up a notch. Be careful, though; these will knock your socks off. Please drink responsibly.

"Don't give in to your fears. If you do, you won't be able to talk to your heart."
—Paulo Coelho

1 fl. oz. vodka
1 fl. oz. tequila
1 fl. oz. rum
1 fl. oz. gin

1 fl. oz. triple sec
1 1/2 fl. oz. sweet and sour mix
Splash cola
1 lime wedge

Procedure

1. Fill a cocktail shaker with ice; pour in vodka, tequila, rum, gin, triple sec, and sweet and sour mix. Cover and shake until the outside of the shaker is frosty.
2. Place a few cubes of ice into a highball glass and strain in the iced tea. Top with the cola and garnish with a wedge of lime.

Yield: 1
Degree of Difficulty: Easy
Preparation Time: 5 minutes
Total Time: 5 minutes

Recipe Type

Beverage

MARGARITA RECIPE

Everybody loves a margarita. The one in this recipe is on the rocks, which I prefer. However, some people prefer them blended, so I've included a recipe for that type as well. To each his own, sweetie.

"A journey of a thousand miles begins with a single step."
—Lao Tzu

Kosher salt
1 thin lime wedge
Ice cubes
1 1/2 oz. tequila

1 oz. triple sec
1/2 oz. freshly squeezed lime juice
1 lime slice

Procedure

1. Cover a small plate with salt. Rub the lime wedge on the outside rim of a 4-ounce cocktail glass. Holding the glass at a 45-degree angle, dip the outside rim in the salt, rotating the glass so the entire rim is coated with salt. Fill the glass with ice and place in the freezer to chill.

2. In a cocktail shaker, add the tequila, triple sec, and lime juice and fill shaker halfway with ice. Shake vigorously until the outside of the container turns frosty. Strain the margarita into the chilled glass and garnish with a lime slice.

Yield: 1 Serving
Degree of Difficulty: Easy
Preparation Time: 5 minutes
Total Time: 5 minutes

Recipe Type

Beverage

PARTY SANGRIA

I didn't know if you've ever had sangria, so I am including a recipe for it. This drink is really easy to throw together, and the recipe makes a big batch, so be sure to invite a crowd over.

"Anger makes you smaller, while forgiveness forces you to grow beyond what you are."
—Cherie Carter-Scott

1 bottle red wine (cabernet sauvignon, merlot, rioja, zinfandel, or shiraz)
1 lemon, cut into wedges
1 orange, cut into wedges
1 lime, cut into wedges
2 Tbs. granulated sugar

Splash orange juice
2 shots triple sec (optional)
1 c. strawberries, fresh or thawed frozen
1 (8-oz.) can diced pineapple (with juice)
4 c. ginger ale

Procedure

1. Pour wine into a large pitcher. Squeeze the juice from the lemon, orange, and lime wedges into the wine.
2. Toss in fruit wedges (leaving out seeds if possible) and pineapple and then add sugar, orange juice, and gin. Chill overnight.
3. Add ginger ale, berries, and ice just before serving.
4. If you'd like to serve right away, use chilled red wine and serve over lots of ice. However, the best sangrias are chilled for around 24 hours in the refrigerator, allowing the flavors to really marinate with each other.

Yield: 12 Servings
Degree of Difficulty: Easy
Preparation Time: 10 minutes
Total Time: 10 minutes

Recipe Type

Beverage

3. BREADS

BEGINNER'S BASIC SOURDOUGH STARTER

Lindsey, dear, you probably remember the days of sourdough in the Gaebel household. There were times when we had 3 quarts growing in the refrigerator at one time. I couldn't bake fast enough to keep up with it. But, oh, how we loved the finished products: bread, pancakes, waffles, rolls, and carrot cake. The list goes on and on, but one day this petered out. Sourdough is good while it lasts, but it takes some work. Should you let your sourdough go bad or let it run out it is easy to start a new batch. Here's the recipe for the starter, in case I don't have any to give you from my supply. It is easy enough to begin, but don't let it get out of hand. The pancakes and other baked goods that can be made from this starter are in the breakfast chapter.

"Fear sells—until you stop buying it."
—Unknown

2 c. warm water

1 package active dry yeast

2 tsp. granulated sugar

2 c. all-purpose flour

Procedure

1. In a medium mixing bowl, add warm water, yeast, and sugar. Mix with wooden spoon until the yeast is dissolved. Set aside for 10 minutes.
2. Stir in flour, mixing until smooth. Pour starter into a plastic container that is at least four times larger than the liquid amount, as the starter will expand. Cover with a cloth napkin held in place with a rubber band. Set the starter in a warm spot for 5 days. Stir each day. After this, refrigerate and use as needed, at least once a week. Replenish with equal amounts of water and flour.

Yield: 24
Degree of Difficulty: Moderately Difficult
Preparation Time: 10 minutes
Cooking Time: 0
Inactive Time: 120 hours
Total Time: 120 hours and 10 minutes

Recipe Type

Bread

BLUEBERRY SURPRISE MUFFINS

These muffins were a favorite of yours when you were growing up. The surprise is the cream cheese in the muffins, and anything with cream cheese is going to be a hit on your list! I had to include it in your cookbook. Bake to your heart's content, my dear!

"Hatred stirs up strife, but love covers all offenses."
—Unknown

1 3/4 c. all-purpose flour
1/3 c. granulated sugar
1 Tbs. baking powder
1 large egg
3/4 c. milk
1/3 c. oil

1 tsp. grated lemon peel
1 (8-oz) pkg. cream cheese, cut into 1/2-
  inch cubes
3/4 c. fresh blueberries
1 tbs. lemon juice
3 tbs. granulated sugar

Procedure

1. Heat oven to 400 degrees F.
2. Mix flour, 1/3 cup sugar, and baking powder in large bowl
3. Beat egg in small bowl; add milk, oil, and lemon peel. Add to flour mixture, stirring just until moistened. Fold in cream cheese and blueberries. Spoon into greased muffin pan, filling each cup 2/3 full.
4. Bake 20 minutes or until lightly browned. Mix juice and 3 tablespoons sugar; brush on muffins before they cool.

Yield: 12 Servings (12 muffins)
Degree of Difficulty: Easy
Oven Temperature: 400°F
Preparation Time: 20 minutes
Cooking Time: 20 minutes
Total Time: 40 minutes

Recipe Type

Bread, Breakfast

BUTTER CRESCENTS

I got this recipe from Judge Caniglia's wife, Malena. She was a wonderful woman, and she loved you so much. Every time we visited her, she gave you something whether it was something to eat, a prayer card, or even a rosary. This recipe has never failed me. The rolls always bring rave reviews, and they freeze beautifully. I'm sure Malena would want you to have this recipe.

"Today I'm thankful for you!"
—Mom

3 3/4 c. all-purpose flour
1 packet active dry yeast
1/3 c. warm water
3/4 c. milk warm
2 large eggs, beaten

4 Tbs. butter, softened
4–5 Tbs. butter, melted
1 tsp. salt
1 1/2 Tbs. granulated sugar

Procedure

1. In a large bowl, mix flour with sugar and salt. In small bowl, dissolve the yeast in the warm water and add to the flour mixture. Add eggs and milk; mix everything together. Add the 4 Tbs. softened butter and knead until the dough is smooth and soft. Cover with a clean dish towel and let it rise for about 1 hour in a warm area, until doubled in size.

2. Punch dough down and divide into 2 equal parts. Form them into balls. On a floured surface, roll each part into a 16- or 17-inch diameter, using a rolling pin. With the back of a spoon, spread about 2 Tbs. of very soft butter onto the dough round. Using a pastry wheel cutter, cut the round into 16 triangles (similar to slicing a pizza). Roll each triangle into crescents, starting from the outside edge. Once rolled, curve the edges and place on a greased baking tray with the tip tucked down and under each roll.

3. Let rolls rise for about 20 minutes. Melt additional 1 1/2 Tbs. butter and brush over the tops of the rolls.

4. Preheat the oven to 400 degrees F (200 degrees C). Bake for 14 to 18 minutes, until puffed and golden brown. Let them cool on a wire rack few minutes before serving.

Yield: 32 Servings
Degree of Difficulty: Moderately Difficult
Oven Temperature: 350°F
Preparation Time: 20 minutes
Cooking Time: 15 minutes
Inactive Time: 1 hour and 20 minutes
Total Time: 1 hour and 55 minutes

Recipe Type

Bread

CHERRY BREAKFAST SCONES

I made these for Curt and myself, and they were delicious. I know how you love scones. These were super easy to make, and they were flaky and yummy. You can whip these up in a jiffy. If you can't find dried cherries, you can substitute dried cranberries.

> "Be better today than you were yesterday."
> —Mom

2 c. all-purpose flour
1/2 c. granulated sugar
1 tsp. baking powder
1/2 tsp. baking soda
1/2 tsp. salt

8 Tbs. unsalted butter frozen
1 (5-oz) pkg. dried cherries
1 large egg
1/2 c. sour cream

Procedure

1. Adjust oven rack to lower middle position and preheat oven to 400 degrees F.
2. In medium bowl, mix flour, 1/3 cup sugar, baking powder, baking soda, and salt. Using on the large holes of a box grater, grate butter into flour mixture; use your fingers to work in butter (mixture should resemble coarse meal.) Then stir in cherries.
3. In small bowl, whisk sour cream and egg together until smooth. Using a fork, stir sour cream mixture into flour mixture until large dough clumps form. Use your hands to scrape the dough away from the sides of the bowl and press into a ball. The dough will be sticky in places and there may not seem to be enough liquid at first, but as you press, the dough will come together. Place on a lightly floured surface and pat into a 7x8-inch circle about 3/4 inches thick. Sprinkle with remaining 1 teaspoon sugar. Use a sharp knife to cut 8 triangles; place on a cookie sheet lined with parchment paper, about 1 inch apart. Bake until golden brown, about 12–15 minutes. Cool for 5 minutes and serve warm or at room temperature.

Yield: 8 Servings
Degree of Difficulty: Very Easy
Oven Temperature: 400 Degrees F
Preparation Time: 15 minutes
Cooking Time: 15 minutes
Total Time: 30 minutes

Recipe Type

Bread

CINNABON CLONE

Who doesn't like the ooey-gooey taste of delicious Cinnabon rolls found that are found in malls or airports? But when they close up shop like they did here, in Omaha, what are you to do but to improvise and try to duplicate the recipe yourself? You loved these as a child, so I found a recipe on the Internet that called for them to be a partially made in a bread machine. Well, that's a dirty word in my household, since I make everything by hand. I converted this recipe to the old-fashioned way, and it turned out beautifully. They're every bit as good as the mall version. Enjoy, my love!

"Doing what you like is Freedom; liking what you do is Happiness."
—Unknown

1 pkg. yeast
1 c. warm milk (110 degrees F)
1/2 c. granulated sugar
1/3 c. butter
1 tsp. salt
2 large eggs, room temperature
4 1/2 c. bread flour
Filling
1 1/4 c. brown sugar, packed

2 1/2 Tbs. cinnamon
1/2 c. butter, softened
Icing
4 Tbl butter, softened
1 1/2 c. powdered sugar
1/4 c. cream cheese, softened
1/2 tsp. vanilla extract
1/8 tsp. salt

Procedure

1. In large bowl, dissolve yeast in warm milk, about 110 degrees F. Stir in sugar and butter. Add, salt, eggs, and flour; mix well. Knead the dough until smooth, about 5 minutes. Cover and set in warm place for about 40 to 60 minutes.
2. After the dough has doubled in size, punch down. Roll out onto well-floured surface until dough measures a 16x21-inch rectangle. It should be about 1/4 inch thick.
3. Preheat oven to 400 degrees F. Lightly grease 9x13-inch baking pan and set aside.
4. To make filling, combine brown sugar and cinnamon in a small bowl.
5. Spread softened butter over entire surface of dough; sprinkle with brown sugar and cinnamon mixture. Working with long edge, carefully roll dough down to bottom edge. Cut dough into 1 3/4 inch slices and set into the prepared pan. Cover pan with towel and let rise 30 minutes or until nearly doubled in size.
6. Bake for 10 minutes or until light golden brown.
7. While rolls are baking, beat together cream cheese, 1/4 cup butter, powdered sugar, vanilla extract, and salt. Beat with electric mixer until fluffy. Spread frosting on warm rolls before serving.

Yield: 12 Servings
Degree of Difficulty: Moderately Difficult
Oven Temperature: 400 degrees F
Preparation Time: 20 minutes
Cooking Time: 10 minutes
Inactive Time: 1 hour and 30 minutes
Total Time: 2 hours

Recipe Type

Bread, Breakfast

CREAM CHEESE BANANA BREAD

This banana bread is your favorite because it's so rich and yummy. I could blindfold you, and you'd still always choose it, hands down. Keep this recipe under lock and key, because it's a winner, sweetheart!

"Watch, stand fast in the faith, be brave, be strong. Let all that you do be done with love."
—1 Corinthians 16:13 NKJV

6 Tbs. unsalted butter softened
4 oz. cream cheese, softened
1 c. granulated sugar
1 large egg
1 1/2 c. all-purpose flour
1/4 tsp. baking powder

1/2 tsp. baking soda
1/2 tsp. salt
3/4 c. bananas, mashed
1/2 c. walnuts, chopped
1 tsp. vanilla extract

Procedure

1. Preheat oven to 350 degrees F. Grease and flour two 8x4-inch loaf pans
2. In large mixing bowl, combine butter and cream cheese. Beat on medium speed with electric hand mixer until creamy. Gradually add sugar, and salt, beating until light and fluffy. Add egg, beating just until combined. Stir together flour, baking powder, and baking soda; gradually add to butter mixture, beating at low speed until just blended. Stir in banana, walnuts and vanilla. Spoon batter into prepared loaf pans.
3. Bake for 1 hour or until a toothpick inserted in center comes out clean and edges of bread pull away from sides of the pan; shield the loaves with aluminum foil for the last 15 minutes if necessary to prevent overbrowning. Cool bread in pans on wire racks for 15 minutes. Remove from pans and cool at least 30 minutes on wire racks before slicing.

Yield: 20 Servings (2 loaves)
Degree of Difficulty: Easy
Oven Temperature: 350 Degrees
Preparation Time: 15 mi
Cooking Time: 1 Hour
Inactive Time: 45 minutes
Total Time: 2 Hours

Recipe Type

Bread

HOLIDAY CRANBERRY NUT BREAD

I remember this being your favorite Christmas bread, second to none, because it was so pretty. You always helped me make both the banana nut and cranberry nut breads for gift-giving at Christmastime. You were always Mommy's helper in the kitchen, so it's no wonder that you love to cook and bake so much today.

"You don't need anyone else's permission to be all God made you to be!"
—Author Unknown

2 c. all-purpose flour
1 c. granulated sugar
1 1/2 tsp. baking powder
1 tsp. salt
1 tsp. baking soda
3/4 c. orange juice

1 Tbs. grated orange peel
2 Tbs. butter
1 large egg
1 (10 1/2-oz.) bag cranberries, frozen then coarsely chopped
1 c. walnuts

Procedure

1. Preheat oven to 350 degrees F. Grease 9x5-inch loaf pan.
2. In medium bowl, mix together flour, sugar, baking powder, salt, and baking soda. Stir in orange juice, orange peel, butter, and egg. Mix until blended well. Stir in cranberries and nuts. Spread evenly in loaf pan.
3. Bake for 55 minutes or until a toothpick inserted in center comes out clean. Cool on a wire rack for 15 minutes. Remove from pan; cool completely. Wrap and store overnight.

Yield: 12 Servings (1 loaf)
Degree of Difficulty: Easy
Oven Temperature: 350°F
Preparation Time: 20 minutes
Cooking Time: 55 minutes
Total Time: 1 hour and 15 minutes

Recipe Type

Bread

PUMPERNICKEL RYE BREAD

Grandma Nell's birthday was March 18, the day after St. Patrick's Day. I don't know if you remember, but when we lived on the farm, I always hosted St. Patty's dinner there for everyone, and the pumpernickel rye I made from scratch was a hit. This is the recipe that I used. Some people don't like the caraway seed, which is optional. If you can find time in your busy schedule, let me know, and I'll give you a lesson in bread making. It will be fun!

"Do small things with great Love."
—Unknown

2 c. warm milk
2 Tbs. vegetable oil
4 Tbs. molasses
3 1/4 c. bread flour
1 1/3 c. rye flour

1/2 c. cornmeal
1 1/4 tsp. salt
1 pkg. active dry yeast
4 Tbs. unsweetened cocoa powder
3 Tbs. brown sugar

Procedure

1. Preheat oven to 375 degrees F.
2. In large mixing bowl, mix the bread flour, rye flour, cornmeal, salt, yeast, cocoa, and brown sugar. Add milk, oil, and molasses. Mix thoroughly. When the dough holds together, knead by hand for 15 to 20 minutes.
3. Cover and let rise in bowl 30 minutes. Punch down, form, and place into 9 1/2x5 inch pan. Cover with damp cloth and let rise about 1 hour. Bake 25 to 30 minutes, covering top with aluminum foil last 10 minutes.

Yield: 12 Servings (1 loaf)
Degree of Difficulty: Moderately Difficult
Oven Temperature: 375°F
Preparation Time: 25 minutes
Cooking Time: 30 minutes
Inactive Time: 1 hour
Total Time: 1 hour and 55 minutes

Recipe Type

Bread

CHEDDAR BAY BISCUITS COPYCAT

I know how much you love the cheddar biscuits at Red Lobster, so I found this copycat recipe online. I changed a couple of ingredients in it, and they taste almost identical to the ones at the restaurant. Hope you try them and love them as much as I do!

> "The Lord will fight for you—you need only be still."
> —Exodus 14:14

2 c. biscuit mix
2/3 c. whole milk, cold
4 Tbs. sharp cheddar cheese, shredded

3 Tbs. butter melted
1/2 Tbs. parsley flakes
1/2 tsp. garlic powder
Pinch salt

Procedure

1. Heat oven to 400 degrees F.
2. Combine biscuit mix, milk, and cheese until a soft dough forms. Drop by spoonfuls onto an ungreased cookie sheet. Bake 6–8 minutes or until golden brown.
3. Mix butter, parsley flakes, garlic powder, and salt. Brush mixture over warm biscuits before removing from cookie sheet.

Yield: 8 Servings
Degree of Difficulty: Easy
Oven Temperature: 375°F
Preparation Time: 10 minutes
Cooking Time: 8 minutes
Total Time: 18 minutes

Recipe Type

Bread

SPICY CORNBREAD

I serve this cornbread with chili. It isn't very spicy, but it has a little bit of a kick to it. You seemed to like it when I've prepared it, so I think Craig will too. You can increase the chili powder if you prefer more spice.

> "In this life we cannot always do great things, but we can do small things with great love."
>
> —Mother Theresa

2 Jiffy cornbread mixes
2 Tbs. chili powder
2 large eggs

2/3 c. whole milk
3 Tbs. sun-dried tomatoes, chopped

Procedure

1. Preheat oven to 350 degrees F.
2. In medium mixing bowl, combine all ingredients and mix until well-incorporated; do not overmix. Coat 8x8-inch baking pan with cooking spray. Spread batter in prepared pan. Bake 20 minutes or until toothpick inserted in center comes out clean.

Yield: 9 Servings
Degree of Difficulty: Easy

Oven Temperature: 350°F
Preparation Time: 10 minutes
Cooking Time: 20 minutes
Total Time: 30 minutes

Recipe Type

Bread

SPROUTED WHOLE WHEAT HEALTH BREAD

I make this bread because of the many kinds of grains it includes. I get them all freshly ground at the nutrition store; this is the freshest, most nutritious bread I have ever made. It is also delicious, which makes the extra effort worthwhile. I want to note how much I love this bread toasted!

> "Real men don't love the most beautiful girl in the world; they love the girl who can make their world the most beautiful.
>
> —Unknown

3 Tbs. active dry yeast
2 3/4 c. warm water (110 degrees F)
3 c. sprouted whole wheat flour
1 c. wheat bran
5 c. bread flour, divided
1 c. wheat germ
1 c. nonfat dry milk

1/2 c. brown sugar
1/2 c. vital wheat gluten
2 Tbs. sesame seeds
1 Tbs. salt
1/4 c. vegetable oil
2 large eggs

Procedure

1. In a small mixing bowl, dissolve yeast in warm water. Let stand until creamy, about 10 minutes.
2. In a large bowl, combine the sprouted whole wheat flour, wheat bran, 3 cups bread flour, wheat germ, milk powder, brown sugar, wheat gluten, sesame seeds, and salt; stir well. Add the yeast mixture, oil, and eggs and stir together.
3. Add remaining bread flour, 1/2 cup at a time, stirring well after each addition. When the dough has pulled together, turn it out onto a lightly floured surface and knead until smooth and elastic, about 8 minutes.
4. Lightly oil a large bowl. Place dough inside and turn to coat with oil. Cover with a damp cloth and let rise in a warm place until doubled in volume, about 1 hour. Punch down the dough and place on a lightly floured surface. Divide the dough into three equal pieces and form into loaves. Place the loaves into three lightly greased 8x4-inch loaf pans. Cover the loaves with a damp cloth and let rise until doubled in volume, about 40 minutes.
5. Preheat oven to 375 degrees F. Bake loaves for 30 minutes or until the top is golden brown and the bottom of the loaf sounds hollow when tapped.

Yield: 36 Servings (3 loaves)
Degree of Difficulty: Moderately Difficult
Oven Temperature: 375°F
Preparation Time: 30 minutes
Cooking Time: 30 minutes
Inactive Time: 1 hour and 40 minutes
Total Time: 2 hours and 40 minutes

Recipe Type

Bread

ZUCCHINI BREAD

This moist and delicious bread is a wonderful compliment to any meal and works great as a breakfast bread. It is a fairly simple recipe, and it is an excellent bread to use as a gift. You may find that you like this bread just as well as banana bread.

"Not all who wander are lost."
—J. R. Tolkien

2 large eggs, beaten
1 1/3 c. granulated sugar
2 tsp. vanilla
3 c. grated fresh zucchini
2/3 c. unsalted butter, melted
2 tsp. baking soda

1/4 tsp. salt
3 c. all-purpose flour
1/2 tsp. nutmeg
2 tsp. cinnamon
1 c. chopped pecans or walnuts (optional)

Procedure

1. Preheat the oven to 350 degrees F (175 degrees C).
2. Butter two 5x9-inch loaf pans. In a large bowl, mix together the sugar, eggs, and vanilla. Stir in the grated zucchini and melted butter. Sprinkle baking soda and salt over the mixture and stir it in. Add the flour, one cup at a time, stirring after each addition. Sprinkle the cinnamon and nutmeg over the batter and mix. Fold in nuts, if using.
3. Divide the batter equally between the loaf pans. Bake for 55 minutes (check for doneness at 50 minutes) or until a wooden pick inserted in to the center comes out clean.

Cool in pans for 10 minutes. Turn out onto wire racks to cool thoroughly.

Yield: 24 Servings (2 loaves)
Degree of Difficulty: Easy
Oven Temperature: 350°F
Preparation Time: 20 minutes
Cooking Time: 55 minutes
Inactive Time: 10 minutes
Total Time: 1 hour and 25 minutes

Recipe Type

Bread, Breakfast

4. BREAKFAST

BREAKFAST CREPES WITH BERRIES

I know how much you love crepes, so I found this recipe for you. These are a winner, so when you try them, invite me over to share them with me.

"The only difference between a good day and a bad day is your attitude."

—Unknown

1 1/2 c. fresh raspberries
1 1/2 c. fresh blackberries
1 c. sour cream
1/2 c. powdered sugar
1 Tbs. lime juice

1 (15-oz) carton orange creme yogurt
1 tsp. grated lime peel
1 tsp. vanilla extract
1/2 tsp. salt
8 crepes

Procedure

1. In a large bowl, combine raspberries and blackberries; set aside. In a small bowl, combine sour cream and powdered sugar until smooth. Stir in the yogurt, lime juice, lime peel, vanilla, and salt. Spread 2 tablespoons of sour cream mixture over each crepe; top with about 1/3 cup berries. Roll up; drizzle with remaining sour cream mixture. Serve immediately.

Yield: 8 Servings
Degree of Difficulty: Moderately Difficult
Preparation Time: 20 minutes
Cooking Time: 20 minutes
Total Time: 40 minutes

Recipe Type

Breakfast, Brunch, Dessert

EASY OVERNIGHT CARAMEL PECAN ROLLS

This is the recipe for the rolls that I would traditionally make the night before Christmas. I knew you wouldn't want to wait to open presents after breakfast, so I always got up early enough to allow these rolls to rise and bake. By the time you got up, they were fresh from the oven. Santa never disappointed you on Christmas morning, and neither did I!

"A friend is a present you give yourself."

—Robert Louis Stevenson

2 c. milk

2 (0.25–oz.) packages active dry yeast

1/2 c. warm water (110 degrees F)

1/3 c. granulated sugar

1/3 c. vegetable oil

1 Tbs. baking powder

2 1/2 tsp. salt

1 egg

7 1/2 c. all-purpose flour

1 1/2 c. packed brown sugar

3/4 c. butter

3 Tbs. light corn syrup

1 1/2 c. pecan halves

1/2 c. butter, softened

3/4 c. white sugar

2 Tbs. ground cinnamon

Procedure

1. Warm the milk in a small saucepan until it bubbles. Remove from heat and let cool until lukewarm. In a small bowl, dissolve yeast in warm water. Let stand until creamy, about 10 minutes.
2. In a large bowl, combine yeast mixture, milk, sugar, oil, baking powder, salt, egg, and 3 cups flour. Beat until smooth. Stir in the remaining flour, 1/2 cup at a time, beating well after each addition. When the dough has pulled together, turn it out onto a lightly floured surface and knead until smooth and elastic, about 8 minutes. Lightly oil a large bowl, place the dough in the bowl, and turn to coat with oil. Cover with a damp cloth and let rise in a warm place until doubled in volume, about 1 hour.
3. Heat brown sugar and 3/4 cup butter until melted. Remove from heat and stir in corn syrup. Divide mixture between two 9x13-inch baking pans. Sprinkle 3/4 cup pecans in each pan.
4. When dough has doubled, punch down and turn out onto a lightly floured surface. Roll out into a large rectangle and spread with softened butter. Sprinkle with sugar and cinnamon. Starting with the long side, roll into a log and slice into 1-inch-wide rolls, 48 in all. Place the rolls slightly apart in pans. Cover with aluminum foil and refrigerate 12 to 48 hours.
5. When ready to bake, remove rolls from refrigerator and let stand in a warm place until doubled in size, about 30 minutes. Meanwhile, preheat oven to 350 degrees F. Bake uncovered in preheated oven until golden, 30 to 35 minutes. Immediately invert pan on heatproof serving plate. Wait 1 or 2 minutes before removing pan so that caramel drizzles over rolls.

Yield: 48 rolls
Degree of Difficulty: Moderately Difficult
Oven Temperature: 350°F
Preparation Time: 30 minutes
Cooking Time: 30 minutes
Inactive Time: 13 hours and 30 minutes
Total Time: 14 hours and 30 minutes

Recipe Type

Breakfast, Bread

EGGS BENEDICT

You loved the eggs Benedict at Village Inn. This is a somewhat tedious recipe, and you need to be able to multitask, but the finished product is simply delicious. I thought you could cook this recipe for me, and I would be the guinea pig. Let me know, honey.

"You are the bows from which your children, as living arrows, are sent forth."

—Gibran

3 whole English muffins
3 slices Canadian bacon
3 large eggs
3 egg yolks

2 sticks butter
1 whole lemon, juiced
Cayenne pepper to taste

Procedure

1. Bring a pot of water to a boil. While waiting for the water to heat, place four English muffin halves and an equal number of Canadian bacon slices on a cookie sheet. Lightly butter the English muffins and place them under the broiler for a few minutes, until the English muffins are very lightly golden. Be careful not to dry out the Canadian bacon.

2. Poach 3 whole eggs by doing the following: With a spoon, begin stirring the boiling water in large, circular motions. When you've formed a whirlpool, crack an egg into the pot. Add the other eggs likewise. Cook for about 2 1/2 to 3 minutes.

3. For the sauce, melt 2 sticks of butter in a saucepan until sizzling. Don't let it burn. Separate three eggs and place the yolks into a blender. Turn the blender on low to allow the yolks to combine, and then slowly pour the hot butter into the blender in a thin stream. The blender should remain on

the whole time. When the butter is added, immediately squeeze lemon juice into the blender. Add Cayenne pepper.

4. Place the English muffins faceup on a plate. Next, place a slice of Canadian bacon on each half. Place the egg on top of the bacon and top with a generous helping of Hollandaise sauce. Note: To ensure that everything is hot when served, plunge the poached eggs back into the hot water just before serving, and make the Hollandaise at the very last minute.

Yield: 3 Servings
Degree of Difficulty: Moderately Difficult
Preparation Time: 30 minutes
Cooking Time: 30 minutes
Total Time: 1 hour

Recipe Type

Breakfast

GERMAN APPLE PANCAKE

Do you remember the morning that you awoke and asked me to make a German apple pancake? I told you I didn't know how to make one. You were only seven or eight years old, and when you persisted, I searched the Internet and came up with this recipe; at 12:30 p.m., we finally sat down to breakfast. Although it was a little late for breakfast, it was worth it because of the look on your face when you tasted it and, because the pancake really was awesome. Thank you, darling Lindsey, for the opportunity to learn how to make an apple pancake. I love you.

"The value of achievement lies in the achieving."
—Albert Einstein

4 large eggs
1/2 c. all-purpose flour
1 tsp. baking powder
2 Tbs. granulated sugar
1 tsp. salt
1 c. whole milk
1 tsp. vanilla extract
2 Tbs. unsalted butter, melted

1 tsp. ground nutmeg
1/2 c. unsalted butter
1/2 c. granulated sugar, divided
1 tsp. ground cinnamon
1 tsp. ground nutmeg
1 medium granny smith apple, peeled, cored, and sliced

Procedure

1. In a large bowl, blend eggs, flour, baking powder, sugar, and salt. Gradually mix in milk, stirring constantly. Add vanilla, melted butter, and 1 teaspoon nutmeg. Let batter stand for 30 minutes or overnight.

2. Preheat oven to 425 degrees F. Melt butter in a 10-inch ovenproof skillet, brushing butter onto the sides of the pan.

3. In a small bowl, combine 1/4 cup sugar, cinnamon, and remaining teaspoon nutmeg. Sprinkle mixture over the buttered pan. Line with apple slices. Sprinkle remaining ¼ cup sugar over apples. Place pan over medium-high heat until the mixture bubbles, and then gently pour the batter mixture over the apples. Bake in preheated oven for 15 minutes. Reduce heat to 375 degrees F and bake for 10 minutes. Slide pancake onto serving platter and cut into wedges.

Yield: 1 German Apple Pancake (4 Servings)
Oven Temperature: 425°F
Preparation Time: 20 minutes
Cooking Time: 25 minutes
Inactive Time: 30 minutes
Total Time: 1 hour and 15 minutes

Recipe Type

Breakfast, Brunch

HEALTHY SWISS MUESLI

After you were born, I went to Diet Center to lose the weight I had gained. One of the breakfast recipes they gave me was for Swiss Muesli, and I fell in love with it. Most people pour milk over it, but I added chopped fresh apple and mixed it with plain yogurt—yummy. When you were old enough to eat solid foods, you ate for breakfast with me. Somewhere along the way, we got away from eating it. Now that I've found the recipe, I think I'll start the ritual again. If you incorporate it into your breakfast too, my dear, you may just love it all over again.

"Remember, men need laughter sometimes more than food."

—Anna Fellows Johnston

3 c. rolled oats
1/3 c. wheat germ
2 Tbs. sesame seeds
2 Tbs. sunflower seeds
1/3 c. almonds, slivered
2 Tbs. canola oil

3 Tbs. honey
1/3 c. dried apricots, chopped
1/3 c. raisins

Procedure

1. Preheat oven to 350 degrees F.
2. Mix oats, wheat germ, sesame seeds, sunflower seeds, and almonds in a large bowl. Add oil and honey to the bowl and stir until well-combined. Pour contents of bowl onto ungreased cookie sheet and create even layer. Bake for 30 to 45 minutes, until the oats and almonds appear golden, stirring well every 10 to 15 minutes to ensure even baking. Once baked, remove cookie sheet from oven and let the oat mixture cool. Once sufficiently cooled, stir in the dried fruit.
3. Store the muesli in an airtight container for up to a month. To serve, I usually mix 1/2 cup of this cereal with 1/4 cup chopped apple and 1/2 cup plain yogurt. It's delicious!

Yield: 12 1/4-cup Servings
Degree of Difficulty: Easy
Oven Temperature: 350°F
Preparation Time: 10 minutes
Cooking Time: 45 minutes
Total Time: 55 minutes

Recipe Type

Breakfast

MAMA'S BUCKWHEAT PANCAKES

Curt and I love this recipe. We use it for waffles as well. The fruit is optional, but we usually include it. This cookbook is mostly filled with recipes of dishes that you grew up with or had some exposure to, but this one is an exception because of the quality and how delicious it is.

> "A loving heart is the truest wisdom."
> —Charles Dickens

1 c. buttermilk
1 large egg
4 Tbs. butter, melted
1/2 c. all-purpose flour
1/2 c. buckwheat flour]

1 tsp. granulated sugar
1/2 tsp. salt
1 tsp. baking soda
3 Tbs. butter
3/4 c. mixed frozen fruit, thawed

Procedure

1. In a medium bowl, whisk together the first three ingredients (egg, buttermilk, and butter). In another bowl, mix together dry ingredients and pour them into the egg mixture. Stir until the two mixtures are just mixed. If desired, thaw fruit and add; stir until just combined.

2. Heat a griddle or large frying pan to medium-hot and add 1 tablespoon of butter, margarine, or oil. Let the butter melt and then spoon batter into the frying pan, forming 4-inch pancakes. Once bubbles form on the tops of pancakes, flip them over and cook on the other side for about 3 minutes. Continue this process until all of the batter has been made into pancakes.

Yield: 6 Servings (12 pancakes or waffles)
Degree of Difficulty: Easy
Preparation Time: 10 minutes
Cooking Time: 10 minutes
Total Time: 20 minutes

Recipe Type

Breakfast

OMELET SUPREME

One thing that is for sure, my daughter loves her eggs for breakfast. Or at least she used to. I haven't checked lately. She and I used to go to Village Inn for breakfast simply because she wanted her eggs and pancakes for breakfast—or lunch—or dinner. Any time of the day was fine with her. This recipe will fit in with your mealtime plan just fine, won't it, Honey? Give it a try. You can make as many substitutions as you would like in this recipe to suit your appetite. Just make it your way.

"We make a living by what we get, but we make a life by what we give."
—Winston Churchill

4 large eggs (or egg substitute equivalent)	1/2 c. mushroom, sliced
1/2 tsp. salt	4 slices bacon, cooked crispy
1/8 tsp. black pepper	2 Tbs. bacon grease
1 c. yellow zucchini, chopped	1/2 c. tomato, chopped
1/2 c. white onion, chopped	1/2 c. cheddar cheese, grated
1 Tbs. fresh garlic clove, minced	1 small tomato, sliced

Procedure

1. Cook bacon until crispy; remove from pan and put on paper towels. Save 2 Tablespoons bacon grease.

2. Cut squash into 1/2-inch slices, and then slice those in quarters. Slice onions, chop garlic, and slice mushrooms. Heat bacon grease and add vegetables (except tomato). Cover with lid and cook on medium-low heat until zucchini is tender and the onions and garlic develop a caramel color. Remove from heat and drain off fat.

3. Break 4 eggs into medium bowl; add salt and pepper. Grease omelet pan with cooking spray and heat pan over medium-low heat. Evenly pour in half of egg mixture, coating the entire bottom of pan, and then cover pan with lid. When the top of omelet no longer looks wet or runny, add tomato along with half of the cheese, half of the vegetable mixture, and 2 slices of bacon. Quickly fold over omelet and cover another minute, just long enough for cheese to melt. Place omelet on plate. Top with fresh slices of tomato. Repeat directions to make second omelet.

4. To avoid under- or overcooking, keep in mind that the outside of the omelet should be tender but not brown.

Yield: 2 Servings
Preparation Time: 15 minutes
Cooking Time: 10 minutes
Total Time: 25 minutes

Recipe Type

Breakfast

SOUR CREAM COFFEE CAKE

I used to make this recipe when you were at St. Stephen's and I was a court reporter. I occasionally substituted the all-purpose flour with whole wheat flour and add a chopped apple to the filling to change things up a bit. It was delicious either way I prepared it, and the recipe got rave reviews. Try this at least once for Craig or for guests; I'm sure it will be a hit.

"All my work is meant to say, 'You may encounter defeats, but you must not be defeated.'"

—Maya Angelou

1 c. granulated sugar
1 c. butter, softened
3 large eggs
2 c. all-purpose flour
1 1/2 tsp. baking powder
1 1/2 tsp. baking soda

1/2 c. sour cream
1 c. walnuts, chopped
3/4 c. granulated sugar
2 tsp. ground cinnamon
1 medium apple, chopped (optional)

Procedure

1. Preheat oven to 350 degrees F. Lightly grease one Bundt pan. In a large bowl, cream together 1 cup of the granulated sugar with 1 cup butter. Add eggs and beat well. Mix in the flour, baking soda, baking powder, and sour cream; stir until just combined.

2. Pour half of the batter into the prepared pan and sprinkle with three-quarters of the filling. Add chopped apple if desired. Pour the remaining cake batter on top and sprinkle with remaining filling. Bake for 40 minutes.

3. To make filling: Combine chopped nuts, ground cinnamon, and 3/4 cup granulated sugar; mix well.

Yield: 12 Servings (1 Coffee Cake)
Degree of Difficulty: Easy
Oven Temperature: 350 Degrees F
Preparation Time: 20 minutes
Cooking Time: 40 minutes
Total Time: 1 hour

Recipe Type

Breakfast, Brunch

SOURDOUGH PANCAKES

These pancakes use the sourdough starter from the bread chapter. You'll remember eating them when you were a child, baby girl. You enjoyed these every week so that I wouldn't kill off my starter. You and your dad both loved them. I hope you'll give the recipe a try; it's well worth the effort.

"Beauty is not in the face; beauty is a light in the heart."
—Kahlil Gibran

2 c. sourdough starter (see bread chapter)
2 Tbs. granulated sugar
1 large egg beaten
4 tsp. vegetable oil

3/4 tsp. salt
1 tsp. baking soda
1 Tbs. water

Procedure

1. In a large bowl, combine the sourdough starter, sugar, egg, oil, and salt; set aside.
2. In a small bowl, dilute 1 teaspoon baking soda in 1 tablespoon of warm water; set aside until ready to cook pancakes.
3. Fold the baking soda-and-water mixture gently into the prepared pancake batter—do not beat. There will be a gentle foaming and rising action in the batter. Let the mixture bubble and foam for a minute or two before using.
4. Heat a lightly greased griddle (cast iron is best) until fairly hot. Pour the batter onto the griddle, using 1/4 cup to 1/2 cup for each pancake.
5. Cook the pancakes 1–2 minutes on each side or until golden brown and bubbly. Remove from heat and serve.

Yield: 4 Servings (8 Pancakes)
Degree of Difficulty: Easy
Preparation Time: 10 minutes
Cooking Time: 10 minutes
Inactive Time: 0

Recipe Type

Breakfast

STRAWBERRY–CREAM CHEESE STUFFED FRENCH TOAST

Strawberries, cream cheese, and french toast—how could you put all three of those components together without saying yum? This is Paula Deen's recipe, from the Food Network, so I thought we could collaborate and see how this comes out. What do you think, darlin'?

> "What you are is what you have been. What you'll be is what you do now."
>
> —Buddha

2 large eggs (or egg substitute equivalent)
1/2 c. milk
1/2 tsp. granulated sugar
1 8-oz. package cream cheese
12 slices white bread, cut up
1 c. sliced fresh strawberries
butter for cooking

Strawberry Syrup
3 c. sliced strawberries
1 c. granulated sugar
Juice of 1 lemon

Procedure

1. In a small bowl, whisk together the eggs, milk, and granulated sugar. Spread the cream cheese on half of the bread slices and top with strawberries. Top with the remaining 6 slices and press around the edges to seal. Melt butter on a griddle over medium-low heat. Dip the sandwiches in the egg mixture for a few seconds on each side. Cook the sandwiches until golden brown, 2–3 minutes per side. Serve with maple syrup, strawberry syrup, or confectioners' sugar.

2. Strawberry Syrup: In a medium saucepan, combine strawberries, sugar, and lemon juice and bring to a boil. Lower the heat and simmer until the strawberries are soft and the syrup is thickened and reduced by 1/3 to 1/2 in volume, 15–18 minutes. Remove from heat and let cool to room temperature before serving. Cook's Note: If thinner syrup is desired, pour the hot syrup through a fine mesh strainer into a clean container and let cool.

Yield: 4 to 6 Servings
Degree of Difficulty: Easy
Preparation Time:10 minutes
Cooking Time: 25 minutes
Total Time: 35 minutes

Recipe Type

Breakfast

5. MAIN DISHES

BARBECUE BRISKET

I made this recipe for work potluck days quite a bit because it is easy and tasty. It was always a hit. The day before I took it to work, I would let it marinate in the liquid smoke, and then it cooked overnight. There was always enough to bring home for dinner too. That's my kind of recipe! It's a keeper, honey!

"Happiness is when what you think, what you say, and what you do are in harmony."
—Mahatma Gandhi

1 5-lb. beef brisket
1 Tbs. salt
1 Tbs. pepper
2 Tbs. meat tenderizer

2 cloves minced garlic
1 (4-oz.) bottle liquid smoke
2 c. barbecue sauce
10 hamburger buns

Procedure

1. Place brisket in large zipper storage bag. Combine remaining ingredients in small bowl and mix well.
2. Pour mixed ingredients into bag, over the brisket. Seal bag and shake to evenly coat brisket.
3. Place in refrigerator for 8 to 10 hours, turning to coat a couple times.
4. When ready to cook, take brisket out of bag and place in slow cooker. Pour 1/4 cup to 1/2 cup of liquid from bag on top of brisket.
5. Cover slow cooker; cook on low for 8 to 10 hours.
6. When ready to serve, shred meat with two forks. Stir in 2 cups of barbeque sauce and mix to combine.
7. Serve on hamburger buns.

Yield: 10 Servings
Degree of Difficulty: Easy
Preparation Time: 10 minutes
Cooking Time: 8 hours
Inactive Time: 12 hours

Recipe Type

Main Dish, Sandwich

BEEF AND NOODLES

This dish has always been a favorite of mine. It isn't an easy recipe, as you make your own noodles, but it's well worth the effort in the end. If you're in a pinch, you can substitute store-bought egg noodles; I would use Reames brand because they're so close that nobody will know the difference. You can let it cook in the slow cooker all day while you're away from home, and when you get back, all you have to do is add the noodles and add a salad or vegetable, and you have a complete meal. It's delicious!

"We must be our own before we can be another's."

—Emerson

1 2-lb. chuck roast
1 Tbs. salt
1 1/2 tsp. pepper
2 tsp. meat tenderizer
2 cloves garlic, minced
2 Tbs. canola oil
4 c. beef broth

Egg Noodles
2 1/2 c. all-purpose flour
1 pinch salt
2 large eggs
1/2 c. milk
1 Tbs. butter

Procedure

1. Early in the day, take roast out and evenly distribute salt, pepper, meat tenderizer, and minced garlic all over surface.
2. In medium skillet, heat canola oil. When skilled is hot, sear all sides of roast.
3. When well-browned, place roast in slow cooker. Cover with beef broth and cover with lid. Turn on low heat.
4. Allow to cook for 8 to 10 hours.
5. For Egg Noodles: in a large bowl, stir together the flour and salt. Add the beaten egg, milk, and butter. Knead dough until smooth, about 5 minutes. Let rest in a covered bowl for 10 minutes.
6. On a floured surface, roll out to 1/8-inch or 1/4-inch thickness. Cut into desired lengths.
7. Allow to air dry before cooking. I make these in the morning right after getting the roast ready, but you may prefer to wait until you get home and let them dry for 30 minutes or so before adding them to the pot.
8. Prior to adding noodles, take two forks and shred roast. Meat is tender enough at this point that this step will be easy.
9. When noodles are dried, add to the crockpot and cover. Allow to cook until noodles are al dente, around 20 minutes.

Yield: 8 Servings
Degree of Difficulty: Moderately Difficult
Preparation Time: 45 minutes
Cooking Time: 8 hours
Total Time: 8 hours and 45 minutes

Recipe Type

Main Dish

BEEF ROULADEN

This is the recipe for Beef Rouladen that I promised you. It is a German dish that I grew up on, and it is very good. Aunt Vicki makes this recipe often. You stuff the beef with bacon and roll it up before you cook it. Grandpa Rich always liked to make this. He put mushrooms in it, but Aunt Vicki does not. The traditional version calls for dill pickle, but Grandpa never did this, so I didn't include it. Serve with mashed potatoes and a vegetable, and you have a full meal.

"Courage is grace under pressure."
—Ernest Hemingway

8 4-oz. pieces of sirloin tip
1/2 c. shallots, finely chopped
2 tsp. salt
2 tsp. freshly ground black pepper

8 slices bacon, cut into halves
2 medium green peppers, chopped
8 bay leaves
3 Tbs. canola oil

Procedure

1. Preheat oven to 350 degrees F.
2. Lay each sirloin tip on workspace. Sprinkle the green pepper, bay leaf, salt, and pepper evenly over the steaks. Lay one slice of bacon and shallots on each piece. Roll the steaks jelly-roll style and secure with toothpicks.
3. Place each roll in roasting pan. Bake at for 1 hour. Remove bay leaf, serve, and enjoy.

Yield: 8 Servings
Degree of Difficulty: Moderately Difficult
Oven Temperature: 350 Degrees F
Preparation Time: 20 minutes
Cooking Time: 1 hour and 10 minutes
Total Time: 1 hour and 30 minutes

Recipe Type

Main Dish, Meat

BEEF WELLINGTON

Do you remember when I first made this recipe for you and your dad and both of you went crazy over it? I served it with asparagus spears and popovers (also included in this cookbook). I told you that this was President Kennedy's favorite meal, and while my recipe varied a bit from the original one, you both fell in love with it. It is not too difficult, and it really is delicious. Now you can make it whenever your heart desires, my love.

> "The only people who are mad at you for speaking the truth are those people who are living a lie. Keep speaking the truth."
>
> —Unknown

4 4-6 oz. beef tenderloin steak	1 (8-oz.) package mushrooms, finely chopped
salt and pepper to taste	2 Tbs. garlic, minced
2 Tbs. olive oil	6 oz. gorgonzola cheese
2 Tbs. butter	1 large sheet puff pastry, chilled
1 medium shallot, finely chopped	1 large egg, beaten

Procedure

1. Heat olive oil in medium skillet on medium-high heat. Sear tenderloins on all sides. Refrigerate until thoroughly chilled.
2. In medium skillet, melt butter. Add shallots, garlic, and mushrooms. Cook until liquid is evaporated. Place in bowl and refrigerate until well-chilled.
3. On well-floured surface, roll puff pastry to 1/4 inch from edge. It will expand as it rises. Roll so that pastry is 2 inches wider than its original size in each direction. With sharp knife, cut pastry into four equal pieces; layer pieces with parchment paper and refrigerate.
4. Preheat oven to 425 degrees F.
5. About 35 or 40 minutes prior to mealtime, remove all ingredients from refrigerator. Place puff pastry on floured surface and place one-quarter of the gorgonzola cheese in center of pastry. Next, place one-quarter of the mushroom mixture on top of cheese and top with tenderloin. Bring one corner of pastry to center of tenderloin and brush top with egg wash. Bring opposite corner and place on first corner; brush with egg wash. Bring other two corners to center of pastry in similar fashion. Pinch pastry to close and seal all edges. Flip package over and place on baking sheet lined with parchment paper. Repeat with other tenderloins. Brush tops with egg wash.
6. Bake in upper third of oven for 20 minutes or until golden brown.

Yield: 4 Servings
Degree of Difficulty: Moderately Difficult
Oven Temperature: 425°F
Preparation Time: 20 minutes
Cooking Time: 20 minutes
Inactive Time: 40 minutes
Total Time: 1 hour and 20 minutes

Recipe Type

Main Dish, Meat

DADDY'S CORNED BEEF AND CABBAGE

Daddy always makes this dish for St. Patrick's Day, and he wanted me to include it in this cookbook. He used to make it for Grandpa and Grandma Gaebel before Grandpa passed away, and they loved to see him bring it for the holiday. He still makes a big deal about it, and he does a good job.

"If you want to be happy, BE."
—Leo Tolstoy

4 lb. corned beef brisket
8 small red potatoes
1 large onion
2 clove garlic
1 small head cabbage

1 lb. carrot
2 bay leaves
2 bottles dark beer
Pickling spice

Procedure

1. Combine all ingredients except pickling spice in large dutch oven. Use spice ball to hang pickling spice from side of dutch oven. Set stove to medium-low and cook for 3 to 3 1/2 hours. Stoves may vary.

Yield: 8 Servings
Degree of Difficulty: Easy

Preparation Time: 15 minutes
Cooking Time: 3 hours and 30 minutes
Total Time: 3 hours and 45 minutes

Recipe Type

Main Dish

GOULASH

I loved eating this as a kid, so I made it often as an adult. You never really said whether you liked it, but I'm including it because you ate it growing up. You could omit the green peppers if you would like to. Either way, it's a good standby dish in my book, and now it is in yours.

"When you stop chasing the wrong things, you give the right things a chance to catch you."

—Author Unknown

2 lb. lean ground beef
2 large yellow onions, chopped
1 green bell pepper, cleaned and chopped
3 cloves garlic, chopped
3 c. water
2 (15-oz.) cans tomato sauce
2 (14.5-oz.) cans diced tomato

3 Tbs. Worcestershire sauce
2 Tbs. Italian seasoning
1 Tbs. chili powder
3 bay leaves
1 Tbs. seasoned salt
2 c. uncooked elbow macaroni

Procedure

1. In a large dutch oven, cook and stir the ground beef over medium-high heat, breaking it up as it cooks, until the meat starts to brown, about 10 minutes. Skim off excess fat and stir in the onions, green peppers, and garlic. Cook and stir the meat mixture until the onions are translucent, about 10 more minutes. Stir in water, tomato sauce, diced tomatoes, Worcestershire sauce, Italian seasoning, bay leaves, chili powder, and seasoned salt. Bring mixture to a boil over medium heat. Reduce to low heat, cover, and simmer 20 minutes, stirring occasionally. Stir in the macaroni, cover, and continue simmering until the pasta is tender, about 25 minutes, stirring occasionally. Remove from heat, discard bay leaves, and serve.

Yield: 8 Servings
Degree of Difficulty: Easy
Preparation Time: 10 minutes
Cooking Time: 1 hour and 5 minutes
Total Time: 1 hour and 15 minutes

Recipe Type

Main Dish, Pasta

MAMA'S BEEF STROGANOFF

I'm including my recipe for the beef stroganoff you often ask for so that you'll always have it close at hand. The fact that you love what I cook for you makes me feel loved. Thank you, baby girl!

"Do not chase people. Be you and do your own thing and work hard. The right people who belong in your life will come to you, and stay."

—Unknown

1 Tbs. olive oil
1 1/2 lb. round steak, cut in large cubes
1 small onion, chopped
1 (8-oz.) package mushrooms, sliced
1 (11-oz.) can cream of mushroom soup
1/2 c. water
1 c. dry red wine

1 Tbs. Beef Base
1/2 c. water
3 Tbs. cornstarch
1 1/2 c. sour cream
6 c. noodles, cooked in salted water and drained (may substitute rice)

Procedure

1. In large skillet, heat olive oil. Add beef and brown on all sides over medium-high heat. Add onion and cook until transparent. Add mushrooms and sauté for 6 to 8 minutes or until somewhat cooked down.

2. In medium bowl, combine soup, water, and wine. Whisk until somewhat smooth. Add to beef mixture in pan and stir to combine well. When heated thoroughly, add beef base and stir to dissolve. Cover and turn heat to low. Let simmer for 1 1/2 hours to allow meat to tenderize.

3. In a 1-cup measure, add 1/2 cup cold water. Add 3 tablespoons cornstarch and mix to dissolve. Turn heat up to medium-high and pour cornstarch mixture into pan, stirring until thickened. Remove from heat. Stir in sour cream and mix well. Serve over hot rice or noodles.

Yield: 6 Servings
Degree of Difficulty: Moderately Difficult
Preparation Time: 15 minutes
Cooking Time: 45 minutes
Total Time: 1 hour

Recipe Type

Main Dish

PIONEER WOMAN'S PRIME RIB WITH ROSEMARY SALT CRUST

I just love Ree Drummond. Her show, *the Pioneer Woman*, has introduced me to wonderful recipes that never let me down. This prime rib is superb. She serves it with Burgundy Mushrooms, which you can find in the side dishes section. Prime rib is for Christmas in my book, so this recipe is extra special. You will need to check the internal temperature of the roast regularly to ensure that it is not overcooked for your preferred doneness.

"Speak from the heart and the truth will be shown."

—Jean Paul-Alice

1 (15-lb.) boneless rib eye roast
2 Tbs. olive oil
1/2 c. minced garlic
1/4 c. tri-color peppercorns

5 sprigs fresh thyme
3 sprigs fresh rosemary
1/2 c. kosher salt

Procedure

1. Preheat the oven to 500 degrees F. Cut the rib eye in half (roast halves separately for more controlled/even cooking). Heat some oil in a large skillet over high heat. Sear both rib eye halves until a nice dark golden color, 2 to 3 minutes per side. Place the peppercorns into a bag and crush with a rolling pin. Shred the leaves from the thyme and rosemary sprigs. Mix the salt with the crushed peppercorns, rosemary leaves, thyme leaves, and garlic. Pour olive oil over the rib eye and pour on the rub mix. Pat slightly to get it to stick to the meat.

2. Roast for 20 minutes, then reduce the heat to 275 degrees F and roast until a meat thermometer registers 125 for rare/medium-rare, about 20 more minutes (the roast will continue to cook slightly after removing from the oven). Remove from the oven and let rest for 15 to 20 minutes before slicing.

Yield: 16 Servings
Degree of Difficulty: Moderately Difficult
Oven Temperature: 500 Degrees F/275°F
Preparation Time: 15 minutes
Cooking Time: 3 hours

Recipe Type

Main Dish, Meat

SIMPLE SIMON SALMON

After my gastric bypass, I had to carefully watch what I ate, and I fell in love with eating salmon. I could choose salmon instead of a steak any day. This recipe is superb. I don't believe I've ever prepared it for you, honey, but you need to try it at least once in your lifetime. It is well worth it.

> "Intelligence without ambition is a bird without wings."
> —Salvadore Dali

3 cloves garlic, chopped
2 Tbs. olive oil
4 (6-oz.) salmon fillets
1/2 c. butter
2 Tbs. Worcestershire sauce

2 Tbs. lemon juice
1/4 c. white wine
1 tsp. ground black pepper
1 tsp. garlic salt
1/4 c. fresh dill, chopped

Procedure

1. Preheat the broiler and set oven rack about 6 inches from the heat source.
2. Line a jelly-roll pan with aluminum foil and spray with nonstick spray. Place garlic and olive oil in a small, microwave safe bowl and cook on high for 1 1/2 minutes. Melt the butter in a saucepan over low heat and stir in the garlic mixture. Remove from heat; stir in the Worcestershire sauce, lemon juice, white wine, black pepper, garlic, and salt. Place the salmon fillets skin-side down on the prepared pan. Spoon about one-third of the butter sauce over the fillets and sprinkle evenly with the fresh dill.
3. Broil for 3 minutes. Turn salmon fillets over and baste with about a third of the remaining butter sauce; broil for 3 more minutes. Turn the fillets again and spoon on the remaining butter sauce; broil until the fish flakes easily with a fork, about 3 additional minutes.

Yield: 4 Servings
Degree of Difficulty: Easy
Preparation Time: 15 minutes
Cooking Time: 6 minutes
Total Time: 21 minutes

Recipe Type

Fish and Shellfish, Main Dish

SWEET BABY SALMON

2 (6-oz.) salmon fillets
2 Tbs. lemon pepper
2 tsp. garlic powder

1/3 c. brown sugar
1/3 c. canola oil
1/3 c. low-sodium soy sauce

Procedure

1. Two and a half hours prior to mealtime, season salmon fillets with lemon pepper and garlic powder.
2. In zipper storage bag, combine brown sugar, canola oil, and soy sauce. Mix well. Place salmon fillets in bag and seal; place in refrigerator for 2 hours.
3. After marinating for two hours, grill salmon fillets over high heat for 3 to 5 minutes on each side; they should be crisp on both sides. Enjoy!

Yield: 2 Servings
Degree of Difficulty: Easy
Preparation Time: 5 minutes
Cooking Time: 10 minutes
Inactive Time: 2 hours
Total Time: 2 hours and 15 minutes

Recipe Type

Main Dish, Seafood

SWEET ORANGE TILAPIA

If you like white fish with a sweeter taste, you will absolutely love this recipe. I always serve it with mixed frozen vegetables and white, wild, or brown rice. It makes a delicious, healthy meal with a quick and easy cleanup. You must try it, honey!

> "Continuous effort—not strength or intelligence—is the key to unlocking your potential."
>
> —Winston Churchill

4 (3-oz.) Tilapia fillets
2 tsp. garlic powder
2 tsp. lemon pepper

1/4 c. brown sugar
4 Tbs. balsamic vinegar
1 (10-oz.) can mandarin oranges

Procedure

1. Drain mandarin oranges, reserving juice.
2. Lay thawed fillets on plate and season with garlic powder and lemon salt. Let sit for 30 minutes.
3. Place fish fillets in zipper storage bag; add balsamic vinegar, brown sugar, and reserved mandarin orange juice. Let marinate for 1 hour.
4. Preheat oven to 350 degrees F.
5. Lay a sheet of foil out and set the fish fillets in the center. Make sure the foil is long enough to accommodate all of the fish. Place oranges over top of fillets; pour half of marinade over fish. Form a packet by folding foil over and crimping the edges. Place packet in preheated oven and bake for 30 minutes.
6. The fish should flake easily with a fork when it is ready. Season to taste with salt and pepper, serve, and enjoy!

Yield: 2 Servings
Degree of Difficulty: Very Easy
Oven Temperature: 350°F
Preparation Time: 10 minutes
Cooking Time: 30 minutes
Total Time: 40 minutes

Recipe Type

Fish and Shellfish, Main Dish

YUM YUMS

This is one of Grandma Nell's recipes that I thought you would like to have. It's a simple version of a sloppy joe that you can throw together at a moment's notice. The recipe calls for using the oven; however, you can easily throw everything in the slow cooker, let it simmer all day, and bring it to a potluck or office party. It's a delicious recipe, and it's a part of Grandma that I thought you would like to have and hand down to your children. It's a way you can keep her close to your heart.

"The real measure of your wealth is how much you'd be worth if you lost all your money."

—Unknown

1 lb. hamburger
1/2 c. milk
2 Tbs. chili powder
Salt and pepper to taste

2 Tbs. dry mustard
1/3 c. catsup
2 Tbs. Worcestershire sauce
1/2 sleeve saltine crackers, crushed

Procedure

1. Preheat oven to 350 degrees F.
2. Combine all ingredients in large mixing bowl. Place in 9x13-inch baking pan and bake 1 hour.
3. Or place in slow cooker for 8 hours on low.

Yield: 8 Servings
Degree of Difficulty: Easy

Oven Temperature: 350°F
Preparation Time: 10 minutes
Cooking Time: 1 hour
Total Time: 1 hour and 10 minutes

Recipe Type

Main Dish, Sandwich

6. SALADS

APPLE JICAMA COLESLAW

You were only about three or four years old when a Baker's supermarket opened in Omaha. It had bigger and better departments than we had seen before, including their produce department. You were amazed by the array of different fruits and vegetables, such as the "ugly vegetable." I explained that it was a jicama, and you wanted to know what it tasted like, so we bought one and took it home. You instantly liked it, and from that day on, every time we visited the produce department, we had to try something new. You were an inquisitive child. I thought you would like to try this coleslaw recipe that calls for jicama and apples. You're still as inquisitive as ever, and I'm sure this dish will pique your curiosity enough for you to give it a whirl.

"A hug is the shortest distance between friends."
—Author Unknown

1/2 small green cabbage, cored and thinly
    sliced
1/2 jicama, cut into 2-inch strips
1 large apple (such as fuji), sliced into matchsticks
3/4 c. mayonnaise
1/2 c. pineapple juice

2 tsp. granulated sugar
Hot sauce to taste
Salt and pepper to taste
1/4 bunch fresh cilantro, chopped
1/3 oz. corn nuts

Procedure

1. Place first three ingredients (cabbage, jicama, and apple) in a large bowl and toss to combine. Whisk mayo, pineapple juice, sugar, hot sauce, salt, and pepper in a bowl until smooth and fluffy, 1 to 2 minutes.
2. Pour mayo mixture over cabbage mixture; toss to combine. Let sit for 5 minutes. Mix in cilantro and toss again. Garnish with toasted corn nuts and serve immediately.

Yield: 8 Servings
Degree of Difficulty: Easy
Preparation Time: 30 minutes
Total Time: 30 minutes

Recipe Type

Salad

SUGAR-FREE CRANBERRY RELISH

This is your favorite dish at any holiday. At our Thanksgiving dinner in 2012 , you rummaged through my refrigerator until you found it, and then you rejoiced with a loud, "Yes!" I have been making this recipe since you were first diagnosed with diabetes at age two, and you have loved it ever since. It is easy to make, and you can keep it close to your heart.

"Life is like an echo: what you send out comes back."

—Chinese Proverb

1 12-oz. bag cranberries, frozen
1 medium apple, tart

1 medium orange
1/2 c. stevia

Procedure

1. Cut apple into 8 pieces; do not seed. Cut orange into 8 pieces; do not peel. Place all of the apple pieces and orange pieces, together with the cranberries, into large bowl of food processor. Pulse until chopped into coarse pieces.

2. Scoop into a medium bowl. Add artificial sweetener and stir until well-incorporated. Refrigerate until ready to serve, at least 2 hours.

Yield: 8 Servings
Degree of Difficulty: Very Easy
Preparation Time: 15 minutes
Inactive Time: 2 hours
Total Time: 2 hours and 15 minutes

Recipe Type

Fruits, Salad

CRISPY GARLIC PARMESAN CROUTONS

I love croutons on my salad. Heck, I love to munch on fresh, homemade croutons. I make croutons from my homemade bread loaves if I don't finish them within a couple of days. These turn out great!

> "We can't change the cards we're dealt, just how we play the hand."
> —Randy Pausch

4 cloves garlic, minced
1/2 c. olive oil
1 8-oz. loaf white bread, cut up
3/4 c. finely grated parmesan cheese

1/2 tsp. italian herbs
1/2 tsp. paprika
1/2 tsp. salt
1/2 tsp. freshly ground black pepper

Procedure

1. Combine the garlic and olive oil in a small mixing bowl. Let sit at room temperature for at least 4 hours to infuse.
2. Preheat oven to 300 degrees F.
3. Cut the bread into 1-inch cubes and add to a large mixing bowl. Add 1/2 cup of the cheese, dried herbs, paprika, salt, black pepper, and cayenne. Strain the garlic oil over the bread cubes, pressing the garlic with the back of a spoon to get every drop of garlicky goodness. Toss with a spatula until the bread is evenly coated.
4. Pour the mixture onto a baking sheet and place in preheated oven for 15 minutes. Remove and stir croutons; the ones on the outside will cook faster than those in the center. Return to oven and bake for 15 more minutes. Remove and sprinkle the last 1/4 cup of cheese over the croutons. Return croutons to oven and bake for 10 to 15 minutes or until browned and crunchy.
5. Allow to cool completely before storing in an airtight container.

Yield: 12 Servings
Degree of Difficulty: Easy
Oven Temperature: 300°F
Preparation Time: 20 minutes
Cooking Time: 45 minutes
Total Time: 1 hour and 5 minutes

Recipe Type

Bread, Salad, Snack

CURT'S FRUIT SALAD

This recipe was handed down to Curt from his mother, and it became a favorite of his. It is light and refreshing and very easy to pull together. We usually have a full bowl in the refrigerator at all times during the late spring and summer months because it is such a favorite. You must give this a try, Lindsey.

> "The purpose of life is a life of purpose."
> —Robert Byrne

4 large apples, cored and diced (Honey Crisp preferred)
3 large oranges, peeled and diced
1 large celery stalk, chopped finely

1 1/2 c. Miracle Whip salad dressing
10 oz. miniature marshmallows

Procedure

1. In medium bowl, combine, apples, oranges, and celery. Add Miracle Whip dressing and stir to mix completely.
2. Add marshmallows and carefully mix. Refrigerate for 2 to 3 hours before serving. Enjoy!

Yield: 12 Servings
Degree of Difficulty: Very Easy

Preparation Time: 20 minutes
Inactive Time: 3 hours
Total Time: 3 hours and 20 minutes

Recipe Type

Salad

GREEK VINAIGRETTE SALAD DRESSING

This is a light salad dressing that you should try. Because it is made with a lot of fresh herbs, you may want to double the recipe and keep it in an airtight container in the refrigerator. By doing this it is more cost efficient and the herbs won't go to waste. If you do this, be sure to use it all within a week. It really is delicious.

"The quieter you become, the more you can hear."
—Unknown

1/4 c. white wine
1/4 c. fresh lemon juice
1 medium shallot, minced
2 tsp. granulated sugar
1 tsp. Dijon-style mustard
2 Tbs. extra virgin olive oil

1 Tbs. fresh dill weed, chopped
2 tsp. fresh oregano, chopped
1 tsp. fresh parsley, chopped
1 tsp. kosher salt
1/4 tsp. black pepper, freshly ground

Procedure

1. In medium bowl, combine wine, lemon juice, shallot, sugar, and mustard; slowly whisk in oil. Next, whisk in herbs, salt, and pepper.
2. Refrigerate at least 1 hour prior to serving.

Yield: 8 Servings
Degree of Difficulty: Very easy

Preparation Time: 10 minutes
Inactive Time: 1 hour
Total Time: 1 hour and 10 minutes

Recipe Type

Salad

HOT GERMAN POTATO SALAD

This is one of Grandpa Rich's recipes. He got it either from Grandma Nell or Grandpa Frank, but he grew up with it and so the story goes. It's different from the potato salad that we're used to because it has no mayo in it and is served hot. It is delicious and worth giving a shot.

"It's kind of fun to do the impossible."
—Walt Disney

4 large red potatoes
4 slices bacon, cooked crispy
1 Tbs. all-purpose flour
2 Tbs. granulated sugar

1/3 c. water
1/4 c. white wine vinegar
1/2 c. chopped green onion
Salt and fresh ground pepper to taste

Procedure

1. Bring large pot of salted water to a boil. Add potatoes; cook until tender but still firm, about 15 minutes. Drain, cool, and chop.
2. Place bacon in a large, deep skillet. Cook over medium-high heat until evenly brown. Drain, crumble, and set aside. Reserve bacon fat.
3. Add the flour, sugar, water, and vinegar to skillet and cook in reserved bacon fat over medium heat until thick.
4. Add bacon, potatoes, and green onions to skillet and stir until coated. Cook until heated; season with salt and pepper. Serve warm.

Yield: 6 Servings
Degree of Difficulty: Easy
Preparation Time: 20 minutes
Cooking Time: 25 minutes
Total Time: 45 minutes

Recipe Type

Salad

MAMA'S GARLIC HOUSE DRESSING

This is my own version of the dressing served at many steak houses, but it has a little more garlic in it, which our family seems to like. It keeps really well in the refrigerator and can be made with either olive oil or canola oil. It is delicious and easy to prepare, and it makes a large batch. The garlic in it is good for you, so how can you go wrong?

"A day of worry is more exhausting than a week of work."
—John Lubbock

4 cloves garlic, minced
1 Tbs. shallot, finely chopped
1/3 c. red wine vinegar
1 1/3 c. canola oil (or olive oil)
1/2 tsp. salt
1/4 tsp. crushed black pepper

1/4 tsp. ground thyme
1/4 tsp. ground rosemary
1/4 tsp. ground basil
1/4 c. grated parmesan cheese (optional)
2 tsp. dijon mustard (optional)

Procedure

1. In a two-cup container that you can easily shake, combine all ingredients and shake well. Refrigerate at least 1 hour prior to serving.
2. To make a french vinaigrette, add 2 teaspoons dijon mustard.

Yield: 25 Servings
Degree of Difficulty: Easy

Preparation Time: 10 minutes
Inactive Time: 1 hour
Total Time: 1 hour and 10 minutes

Recipe Type

Salad

RAMEN BROCCOLI COLE SLAW (WEDDING SALAD)

This salad has been served at almost every wedding we've attended on my side of the family, hence the name. The ramen noodles along with the broccoli coleslaw mix give it a crunch. So, when someone asks for the recipe for the wedding salad, you can tell them that you have it, sweetheart.

"Do a little more each day than you think you possibly can."

—Lowell Thomas

2 (3-oz.) package beef-flavored ramen noodles
2 (8 1/2 oz.) pkg. broccoli coleslaw mix
1 c. toasted slivered almonds
1 c. sunflower seeds

1/2 bunch green onion, chopped
1/2 c. sugar
3/4 c. canola oil
1/3 c. white vinegar

Procedure

1. Before opening noodles, crush into 1-inch pieces. Open packages and set aside flavor packets.
2. Place noodles in bottom of large serving bowl. Top noodles with broccoli slaw; sprinkle with almonds, sunflower kernels, and green onions.
3. In a separate bowl, combine sugar, oil, vinegar, and flavor packets from noodles. Pour over slaw, and then cover and chill up to 24 hours. Toss before serving.

Yield: 1 Serving (82 g)
Degree of Difficulty: Easy
Preparation Time: 15 minutes
Inactive Time: 12 hours
Total Time: 12 hours and 15 minutes

Recipe Type

Salad

BLUE CHEESE DRESSING

I just love a blue cheese dressing, and this is about the best recipe I've come up with so far. It's rich, thick, and delicious. If you want a thinner dressing, whip it until you get a thinner consistency. I like this recipe because of the cream cheese, which makes it that much more flavorful. However, it is not ideal for the diet-conscious. This recipe is a winner, my love.

"Those who wish to sing, always find a song."

—Swedish proverb

6 ounces cream cheese, softened
4 Tablespoons mayonnaise
3/4 cup sour cream
2 teaspoons minced garlic

salt and pepper to taste
1 Tablespoon lemon juice
3 Tablespoons milk
1 1/2 ounces blue cheese

Procedure

1. In medium bowl, stir together cream cheese, mayonnaise, sour cream, garlic, and salt and pepper. Mix in lemon juice and milk, stirring until smooth. Crumble blue cheese into mixture and fold into mix without breaking up chunks.

Yield: 10 Servings
Degree of Difficulty: Easy
Preparation time: 10 minutes
Cooking time: 0
Total Time: 10 minutes

SEAFOOD PASTA SALAD

Summertime brings thoughts of pasta salads, especially seafood pasta salads. This easy and delicious version is a favorite of mine. The tricolor pasta makes it pretty, and it tastes so fresh with the frozen peas and crunchy celery. I hope you will like this recipe too.

"It is never too late to be what you might have been."
—George Eliot

12 oz. tricolor pasta (rotini)
4 stalks celery, chopped
1 lb. imitation crabmeat
1 c. frozen green peas
1 c. mayonnaise
2 Tbs. white sugar

2 Tbs. white vinegar
3 Tbs. milk
1 tsp. salt
1/2 tsp. ground black pepper
1 (8-oz.) package small shrimp, peeled and
   deveined

Procedure

1. Bring a large pot of lightly salted water to a boil. Add pasta and cook for 8 to 10 minutes or until al dente; drain and rinse under cold water until cooled. While pasta is cooking, chop celery, crabmeat, and shrimp. Run hot water over peas to defrost. In a large bowl, whisk together the mayonnaise, sugar, vinegar, milk, salt, and pepper.

2. Add the pasta, celery, and crabmeat, stirring until evenly coated. Adjust the salt, sugar, or mayonnaise to suit your taste. Chill several hours before serving.

Yield: 8 Servings
Degree of Difficulty: Easy
Preparation Time: 15 minutes
Cooking Time: 25 minutes
Inactive Time: 3 hours
Total Time: 3 hours and 40 minutes

Recipe Type

Main Dish, Pasta, Salad, Seafood

STRAWBERRY PRETZEL SALAD

You've always loved this dish. In the past, I have made some substitutions to so that it's diabetic-friendly; this is easy to do if you wish. The salad is one of my favorites too. Now you'll be able to find it easily and make it whenever you wish.

> "We don't stop playing because we grow old; we grow old because we stop playing."
> —George Bernard Shaw

2 c. crushed pretzels
3/4 c. butter melted
3 Tbs. granulated sugar
1 (8-oz.) package cream cheese, softened
1 c. granulated sugar

1 (8-oz.) carton frozen whipped topping, thawed
1 (6-oz) pkg. strawberry gelatin
2 c. boiling water
2 (10-oz.) package frozen sweetened strawberries

Procedure

1. Preheat oven to 400 degrees F.
2. Stir together crushed pretzels, melted butter, and 3 tablespoons granulated sugar; mix well and press mixture into bottom of 9x13-inch baking dish. Bake 8–10 minutes, until set; put aside to cool.
3. In large mixing bowl, cream together cream cheese and granulated sugar. Fold in whipped topping. Spread mixture onto cooled crust. Dissolve gelatin in boiling water; stir in frozen strawberries and allow to set. When mixture is about the consistency of egg whites, pour and spread over cream cheese layer. Refrigerate until set.

Yield: 24 Servings
Degree of Difficulty: Easy
Oven Temperature: 400°F
Preparation Time: 20 minutes
Cooking Time: 10 minutes
Inactive Time: 3 hours
Total Time: 3 hours and 30 minutes

Recipe Type

Salad, Dessert

TACO SALAD

Some people may categorize this as a main dish, but I chose to put it under salads. The nice thing is that you can add or exclude almost any items, and a taco salad will still taste great. I know how much you love Frito's, honey, so you can easily substitute them for the tortilla chips. For the salad dressing, you can substitute a Catalina-type dressing; I prefer to use salsa. You can also substitute black beans for the kidney beans if you wish. Just add whatever you want—the sky's the limit. Enjoy!

"What can you do to promote world peace? Go home and love your family."
—Mother Theresa

1 lb. lean ground beef
1 Tbs. chili powder
2 c. low-fat salad dressing (Miracle Whip)
1 c. catsup
1 (1 1/4-oz.) pkg. taco seasoning mix
1 head iceberg lettuce, rinsed, dried, and chopped
1 head romaine lettuce, rinsed, dried, and chopped
3 large tomatoes, diced
1 green bell pepper, diced

1 yellow or red bell pepper, diced
1 bunch green onion, chopped
1 (4-oz.) can green chile peppers, finely chopped
1 (15-oz.) can kidney beans, drained
1 (15-oz.) can garbanzo beans, drained
12 oz. shredded cheddar cheese
1 (14.5-oz.) pkg. corn tortilla chips
Sour cream as desired
Guacamole as desired

Procedure

1. Brown the beef, and then drain it and season with chili powder; set aside to cool. Prepare the dressing by whisking the Miracle Whip, catsup, and taco seasoning mix together in a small bowl. In a large bowl, combine iceberg lettuce, romaine lettuce, tomatoes, green pepper, red or yellow pepper, green onions, jalapeno peppers, kidney beans, garbanzo beans, half of the cheese, half of the crushed chips, dressing, and cooled ground beef. Mix well, cover, and refrigerate. Just before serving, top the salad with the other half of the cheese and crushed chips.

Yield: 12 Servings
Degree of Difficulty: Easy
Preparation Time: 30 minutes
Inactive Time: 3 hours
Total Time: 3 hours and 30 minutes

Recipe Type

Salad, Main Dish

THOUSAND ISLAND DRESSING

If you would like to get on Daddy's good side, all you have to do is make him a good version of Thousand Island dressing. He loves it. This is a good recipe, and it is a cinch to whip up. Next time you have him over for soup and salad, try this out on him. You may be surprised!

"The greatest thing you'll ever learn is just to love and be loved in return."
—Unknown

1 c. mayonnaise
1/4 c. catsup
1/4 c. chili sauce
1/4 c. sweet pickle relish

1 tsp. salt
1 tsp. ground black pepper
2 green onions, chopped finely
1 Tbs. granulated sugar

Procedure

1. In a small bowl, mix together the mayonnaise, catsup, relish, chili sauce, pickle relish, green onions, sugar, salt, and pepper until thoroughly combined. Refrigerate for at least 2 hours prior to serving; refrigerate leftovers.

Yield: 6 Servings
Degree of Difficulty: Easy
Preparation Time: 10 minutes
Inactive Time: 2 hours
Total Time: 2 hours and 10 minutes

Recipe Type

Salad

7. SIDE DISHES

CALICO BAKED BEANS

This wonderful recipe calls for four different types of beans. It requires an entire package of bacon as well. This is one of my favorite recipes for baked beans. It is a keeper to use as a side dish for barbecues in the summer; keep it close, honey.

"The way I see it, if you want the rainbow, you gotta put up with the rain."
—Dolly Parton

1 (15-oz.) can kidney beans, drained
1 (15-oz.) can butter beans, drained
1 (15-oz.) can northern beans, drained
2 (15-oz.) cans pork and beans
1/2 pound bacon
1 small onion, diced

2 cloves garlic, minced
1/2 tsp. dry mustard
1/2 c. vinegar
3/4 c. brown sugar
1/4 c. molasses
1/2 c. catsup

Procedure

1. Brown bacon and onion. Drain fat and chop bacon in large pieces.
2. In 2-quart pan, add all ingredients except beans. Simmer for 20 minutes.
3. Drain kidney beans, butter beans, and northern beans; mix with pork and beans in a 2-quart ceramic casserole.
4. Pour mixture over beans; mix well and bake uncovered at 350 degrees for 1 hour and 15 minutes.

Yield: 12 Servings
Degree of Difficulty: Easy
Oven Temperature: 350°F
Preparation Time: 15 minutes
Cooking Time: 1 hour and 15 minutes
Total Time: 1 hour and 30 minutes

Recipe Type

Side Dish

CAULIFLOWER MAC-AND-CHEESE CASSEROLE

Because of your diabetes and my hypoglycemia, we both have to watch our diets. I got the idea of making this dish from a friend. The first time I served it, you couldn't get enough of it. It brought tears of happiness to my eyes because it didn't raise your blood sugar and was actually good for you. Now that you have the recipe, you can whip up a batch as often as you want to. Love you!

"It is the heart always that sees before the head can see."

—Thomas Carlyle

1 head cauliflower, cut into small florets
2 c. heavy cream
1 1/2 tsp. dry mustard
1/2 lb. monterey jack cheese, coarsely grated

2 c. grated parmesan
6 oz. goat cheese cut into small pieces
Salt to taste
Freshly ground pepper to taste

Procedure

1. Preheat oven to 400 degrees F. Stir dry mustard into heavy cream.
2. Layer the cauliflower, heavy cream, and 3 cheeses in a medium casserole dish. Season with salt and pepper. Roast for 20 to 30 minutes or until cauliflower is soft and the sauce has thickened slightly.
3. Remove from the oven and let rest for 10 minutes before serving. Cook's Note: Recipe can be doubled and made in a roasting pan if desired.

Yield: 6 Servings
Degree of Difficulty: Easy
Oven Temperature: 375°F
Preparation Time: 20 minutes
Cooking Time: 15 minutes
Total Time: 35 minutes

Recipe Type

Side Dish, Vegetables

CLASSIC CREAMED SPINACH

I remember how much you loved this when I made it, and you should enjoy it for the health benefits alone. It's easy to make and good for you. It tastes similar to the creamed spinach that we used to get from Boston Market, which I know that you liked. So keep this recipe around to make often.

"If you want to understand today, you have to search yesterday."
—Pearl Buck

3/4 lb. fresh spinach, torn
2 Tbs. olive oil
6 Tbs. butter, cubed
3 large cloves garlic, minced
1/4 c. onion, chopped
1/4 c. all-purpose flour

1/2 tsp. salt
1/8 tsp. ground nutmeg
3/4 c. whole milk
3/4 c. heavy cream
1/2 c. parmesan cheese, freshly grated

Procedure

1. In a dutch oven, cook spinach in oil for 3 minutes or until wilted. Transfer to a cutting board; chop.
2. Melt butter in the dutch oven. Add onion and garlic; sauté for 2 minutes or until crisp-tender. Stir in flour, salt, and nutmeg until combined. Gradually whisk in milk and heavy cream until blended. Bring to a boil; cook and stir for 2 minutes or until thickened.
3. Return spinach to dutch oven and add parmesan cheese. Stir well and serve while hot.

Yield: Yield: 4 Servings
Degree of Difficulty: Easy
Preparation Time: 5 minutes
Cooking Time: 20 minutes
Total Time: 25 minutes

Recipe Type

Side Dish, Vegetables

CORN AND OYSTER CASSEROLE

This recipe is from Curt's collection, and you tried it this past Thanksgiving. You said that you liked it, so I'm including it in this cookbook. It's an easy recipe, and it tastes very good. Now you can pass it down to your children, honey.

"Children require guidance and sympathy far more than instruction."
—Annie Sullivan

1 15-ounce can cream-style corn
1 8-ounce can oysters
1 large egg
1/2 c. milk

3 Tbs. butter
1/2 c. heavy cream (optional)
Salt and pepper to taste
1 c. saltine crackers, crushed

Procedure

1. Preheat oven to 350 degrees F.
2. Mix all ingredients together in a 1-quart casserole and dot liberally with butter. To make it extra rich and tasty, add 1/2 cup cream to casserole about 10 minutes before done. Bake for 30 to 40 minutes.

Yield: 8 Servings
Degree of Difficulty: Easy

Oven Temperature: 350°F
Preparation Time: 10 minutes
Cooking Time: 30 minutes
Total Time: 40 minutes

Recipe Type

Side Dish, Vegetables

CREAMED CORN LIKE NO OTHER

I'd never tried creamed corn, even the canned variety, before I met Curt. This recipe, however, leaves canned cream corn in the dust. It is thick, creamy, and rich! Once you try this version, you'll never go back to the canned version again!

Jesus replied, "What is impossible with men is possible with God."
—Luke 18:27 NKJV

2 (10-oz.) pkg. frozen corn kernels, thawed
1 c. heavy cream
1 tsp. salt
2 Tbs. granulated sugar
1/4 tsp. freshly ground black pepper

2 Tbs. butter
1 c. whole milk
2 Tbs. all-purpose flour
1 c. freshly grated parmesan cheese

Procedure

1. In a skillet over medium heat, combine the corn, cream, salt, sugar, pepper, and butter.
2. Whisk together the milk and flour; stir into the corn mixture. Cook over medium heat, stirring until the mixture is thickened and corn is cooked through.
3. Remove from heat and stir in the parmesan cheese until melted. Serve hot.

Yield: 8 Servings
Degree of Difficulty: Easy
Preparation Time: 5 minutes
Cooking Time: 15 minutes
Total Time: 20 minutes

Recipe Type

Side Dish, Vegetables

DELICIOUS DILL POTATO SALAD

This potato salad is healthier because it doesn't take as much mayo as other recipes. The dill adds a distinct flavor not found in other recipes, and I really like it. This recipe is truly worth trying, because it is delicious. It makes a really pretty salad.

"The best gifts come from the heart, not the store."
—Sarah Dessen

3 lb. new potatoes, scrubbed and quartered
2/3 c. italian salad dressing
1 c. mayonnaise
1/2 c. chopped green onion

4 tsp. chopped fresh dill
2 tsp. dijon mustard (optional)
2 tsp. lemon juice
1/4 tsp. pepper

Procedure

1. Bring a large pot of water to a boil. Add potatoes and cook for about 10 minutes or until tender. Drain and set aside to cool.
2. Meanwhile, in a large bowl, stir together the salad dressing, mayonnaise, green onions, dill, mustard, lemon juice, and pepper.
3. When the potatoes are cooled, add to bowl and stir until coated. Refrigerate for a couple of hours to allow flavors to blend before serving.

Yield: 12 Servings
Degree of Difficulty: Easy
Preparation Time: 15 minutes
Cooking Time: 20 minutes
Inactive Time: 2 hours
Total Time: 2 hours and 35 minutes

Recipe Type

Potatoes, Pasta, and Grains, Salad, Side Dish, Vegetables

HASH BROWN CASSEROLE

I got this recipe from Aunt Mary Lou, and it always gets rave reviews. It's a cinch to whip up, and it's very tasty. If you wish, you can refrigerate it overnight and then bake it the next day when you're ready to serve it. It also gives you something to hold onto from someone you love.

"To be trusted is a greater compliment than to be loved."

—George MacDonald

1 (30-oz.) package frozen hash brown potatoes, thawed
2 c. sour cream
1 10.5-ounce can cream of mushroom soup
2 c. grated cheddar cheese
1/2 c. onion, finely chopped
1 tsp. salt
1/2 c. butter, melted
2 c. cornflakes, crushed

Procedure

1. Grease a 9x13-inch baking dish. Heat oven to 350 degrees F.
2. In a large bowl, combine thawed potatoes, sour cream, soup, 1 cup of cheese, onions, salt, and pepper.
3. Top with crushed cornflakes and pour melted butter over top. Top with remaining cheese.
4. Bake for 25 to 35 minutes, until hot and lightly browned. .

Yield: 12 Servings
Degree of Difficulty: Easy
Oven Temperature: 350°F
Preparation Time: 15 minutes
Cooking Time: 30 minutes
Total Time: 45 minutes

Recipe Type

Side Dish, Vegetables

MAMA'S SWEET POTATO SOUFFLÉ

I was afraid to make this recipe because it didn't call for our beloved marshmallows. I hesitantly threw this and that together by reading the ingredients from several different recipes. This is the result, and it was a hit during Thanksgiving 2012 I think it's become a new family favorite.

"To learn and never be filled, is wisdom; to teach and never be weary, is love."
—Unknown

3 c. sweet potatoes, mashed
1 c. granulated sugar
1/2 c. butter, melted
2 large eggs, beaten
1 tsp. vanilla extract
1/2 c. milk

Topping
1 c. brown sugar
1/2 c. all-purpose flour
1/3 c. butter, melted
1 c. chopped pecans

Procedure

1. Preheat the oven to 350 degrees F.
2. Filling: In a large bowl, combine the filling ingredients. Transfer to a buttered 1 1/2 quart casserole.
3. Topping: In a medium bowl, combine the brown sugar, flour, and butter until they are moist and the mixture clumps together. Stir in pecans and spread over sweet potatoes in an even layer. Bake until the top is golden, about 25–30 minutes. Remove from oven and serve hot.

Yield: 12 Servings
Degree of Difficulty: Easy
Oven Temperature: 350 Degrees
Preparation Time: 15 minutes
Cooking Time: 30 minutes
Total Time: 45 minutes

Recipe Type

Potatoes, Pasta, and Grains, Side Dish

RESTAURANT-STYLE FRIED RICE

I know how much you love fried rice from Chinese restaurants, so I've included a recipe that you can prepare at home easily. It tastes just like you would find at a restaurant, and you can prepare it in the convenience of your humble abode. The next time you have the appetite for fried rice, just reach for your cookbook and whip up your own batch!

"Good things happen when you meet strangers."
—Yo-Yo Ma

3 c. white rice
4 c. water (for rice)
1 1/2 c. frozen peas and carrots
3 Tbs. vegetable oil

2 large eggs
Soy sauce to taste
Sesame oil to taste (optional)

Procedure

1. In a medium saucepan, combine rice and water. Bring to a boil. Reduce heat, cover, and simmer for 20 minutes.
2. In a small saucepan, boil peas and carrots for 3 to 5 minutes. Drain.
3. Heat wok or large skillet over high heat. Pour in oil, and then stir in the carrots and peas; cook about 30 seconds. Crack in eggs, stirring quickly to scramble them with vegetables. Stir in cooked rice. Shake in soy sauce and toss rice to coat. Drizzle with sesame oil if desired and toss again.

Yield: 8 Servings
Degree of Difficulty: Moderately difficult
Preparation Time: 15 minutes
Cooking Time: 30 minutes
Total Time: 45 minutes

Recipe Type

Side Dish

TWICE BAKED POTATOES

These are delicious with a good steak dinner. They are somewhat tedious to make; however, they are worth it. The scallions and bacon crumbles on top make them quite pretty as well.

> "Every man dies. Not every man really lives."
> —Braveheart

6 russet potatoes
Olive oil
1 1/2 c. shredded cheddar cheese plus
   1/2 c. for topping
3/4 c. sour cream
3/4 c. half-and-half

1/4 c. (1/2 stick) unsalted butter, softened
1 bunch scallions, chopped
3 slices bacon, cooked crisp and crumbled
Kosher salt and freshly cracked black pepper

Procedure

1. Preheat the oven to 400 degrees F.
2. Scrub the potatoes and dry thoroughly. Drizzle with olive oil, coating evenly. Bake on a sheet pan until the skin is crispy and the potatoes are cooked through, about 1 hour. Allow to cool slightly on a wire rack.
3. Slice each potato in half lengthwise. Using the tip of a spoon, scoop out the flesh into a mixing bowl. Leave about a quarter inch of flesh lining each potato skin. Transfer the potato skins back to the baking sheet and return to the oven for 8 minutes.
4. In the meantime, mash the potato flesh with a fork and add the cheese, sour cream, half-and-half, and butter. Stir in the scallions and bacon (reserving some for garnish) and season with salt and pepper. Remove the potato skins from the oven and set the temperature to broil.
5. Working carefully with the hot potatoes, use a spoon to evenly fill each shell with the potato mixture and top with the additional cheese. Place in oven until the cheese has melted and the potatoes are crisp on top, 3 to 5 minutes. Garnish with the reserved scallions and bacon bits.

Yield: 6 Servings
Degree of Difficulty: Moderately Difficult
Preparation Time: 25 minutes
Cooking Time: 1 hour
Total Time: 1 hour and 25 minutes

Recipe Type

Potatoes, Pasta, and Grains, Side Dish, Vegetables

8. SOUPS AND STEWS

BEEF BARLEY SOUP

Although this recipe is not Lindsey-tested, it is a favorite of mine. I love this soup on a cold winter's night. It's full of big pieces of stew meat, tomatoes, and carrots, and I love barley. You've got to try this recipe at least once to see if it becomes a favorite of yours too, sweetie!

> "Too many people undervalue what they are and overvalue what they're not."
> —Unknown

7 c. water
3 Tbs. Better Than Bouillon Beef Base
1 lb. beef stew meat, cut into 1/2-inch chunks
1 Tbs. canola oil
2 large onions, chopped
1 lb. sliced fresh mushrooms

4 medium carrots, sliced
1 (14 1/2-oz.) can diced tomato, drained
1/2 tsp. salt
1/2 tsp. black pepper
1 c. quick-cooking pearl barley

Procedure

1. In a soup pot, sear the stew meat in 1 tablespoon vegetable oil until browned on all sides. Combine all other ingredients except the barley; cover and bring to a boil over high heat.
2. Reduce heat to low. Cover and simmer for 1 to 2 hours, stirring occasionally. Add barley and simmer for 15 to 20 minutes or until the barley is tender.

Yield: 6 Servings
Degree of Difficulty: Easy
Preparation Time: 10 minutes
Cooking Time: 2 hours
Total Time: 2 hours and 10 minutes

Recipe Type

Main Dish, Soups

CHICKEN TORTILLA SOUP

As you know, my dear daughter, I love eating Mexican food; my new favorite is tortilla soup. This Chicken Tortilla Soup recipe is outstanding. Give it a try when you're in the mood for a Tex-Mex dish.

> "Beautiful in my opinion has nothing to do with looks. It's how you are as a person and how you make others feel about themselves."
>
> —The Notebook of Life

3 Tbs. butter
1 Tbs. minced garlic
1 medium onion, finely chopped
3 Tbs. all-purpose flour
6 c. water
3 Tbs. Better Than Bouillon Chicken Base
3 c. half-and-half
1 (10.75-oz.) can cream of chicken soup
1 c. salsa, mild or medium
1 rotisserie chicken, shredded
1 (15-oz.) can black beans, drained

1 (15-oz.) can kidney beans, drained
1 (15-oz.) can whole kernel corn, drained
2 1/2 tsp. ground cumin
1 (1.27-oz.) packet fajita seasoning
1 bag tortilla chips
8 oz. monterey jack, grated
8 oz. sharp cheddar, grated
1 medium avocado, cut into 1/2-inch chunks
1 c. sour cream

Procedure

1. Melt the butter in a large pot over medium heat. Add the garlic and onion and sauté until softened, about 5 minutes. Add the flour and stir well, cooking for 1 minute more.
2. Add the water, bouillon, and half-and-half. Stir in the cream of chicken soup, salsa, shredded chicken, beans, corn, cumin, and fajita seasoning. Simmer over low heat for 15 minutes.
3. Crumble the tortilla chips into individual bowls and top with a ladleful of soup. Sprinkle each serving with cheese and add a dollop of sour cream and avocado pieces.

Yield: 8 Servings
Degree of Difficulty: Easy
Preparation Time: 15 minutes
Cooking Time: 25 minutes
Total Time: 40 minutes

Recipe Type

Main Dish, Soups

DADDY'S OYSTER SOUP

I believe Daddy's all-time favorite food is this oyster soup. He makes it whenever he can get oysters, usually around Christmastime. He would eat it every day of the week if he could. He insisted on including this in your cookbook.

"What we need even more than foresight or hindsight is insight."
—Unknown

1/2 gallon whole milk
2 pints oysters

1/4 stick butter
Salt and pepper to taste

Procedure

1. Warm milk to medium heat. Add oysters and turn heat to low. Stir occasionally. Do not let milk boil. Add butter and stir until melted. Add salt and pepper to taste. Heat until hot but not to boiling point. Enjoy.

Yield: 6 Servings
Degree of Difficulty: Easy

Preparation Time: 10 minutes
Cooking Time: 20 minutes
Total Time: 30 minutes

Recipe Type

Main Dish, Seafood, Soups

EGG DROP SOUP

Here's an easy version of this soup that you can make at home instead of going out to a Chinese restaurant. I thought your cookbook wouldn't be complete without it, my dear.

"To be surprised, to wonder, is to begin to understand."

—José Ortega y Gasset

4 c. chicken stock
3 large eggs
1/2 tsp. grated ginger
1 Tbs. cornstarch

1 Tbs. soy sauce
3 green onions (scallions), sliced
1/2 tsp. white pepper
3/4 c. Shiitake mushrooms, thinly sliced

Procedure

1. In a bowl, mix 1/2 cup cold chicken stock with cornstarch; set aside.
2. Place remaining stock, onions, mushrooms, green onions, soy sauce, ginger, and white pepper in a pot and bring to a boil. Add cornstarch and stock mixture; stir to thicken. Reduce heat to a simmer.
3. Slowly stir beaten eggs into stock; they will form ribbons. Turn off heat and garnish with a few more green onions.

Yield: 4 Servings
Degree of Difficulty: Easy
Preparation Time: 5 minutes
Cooking Time: 30 minutes
Total Time: 35 minutes

Recipe Type

Side Dish, Soups

HAM AND BEAN SOUP

I like this recipe because even though you cook the ham, bacon, and leeks in a skillet, you finish the soup by putting it in a slow cooker all day. The flavors meld, and it becomes so good. It's a delicious recipe that you should give a try, Lindsey.

"Creativity requires the courage to let go of certainties."
—Erich Fromm

1 lb. dried great northern beans, sorted and rinsed
4 c. water
1/4 c. celery, chopped
1 small onion, chopped
2 bay leaves
1/4 tsp. ground cumin
1/2 tsp. garlic powder
1 tsp. dried parsley

1 Tbs. butter
1 Tbs. olive oil
2 leeks (bulb only), cut in half lengthwise
1 lb. cooked ham, cut into bite-size pieces
5 slices bacon
4 c. chicken stock
1 pinch sea salt (to taste)
1 pinch fresh ground black pepper (to taste)
1 Tbs. black peppercorns

Procedure

1. Place the beans into a large container and cover with several inches of cool water; let stand 8 hours to overnight. Drain and rinse before using.
2. Combine the soaked beans, 4 cups of water, celery, onion, bay leaves, cumin, garlic powder, and parsley in a slow cooker.
3. Melt the butter with the olive oil in a skillet over medium heat; stir in the leeks and cook until tender and smaller pieces start to brown, 8 to 10 minutes. Transfer the leeks to the slow cooker.
4. In the same pan, cook the ham, stirring occasionally, until the edges start to brown; add to soup mixture in slow cooker. Place the bacon into the hot skillet and panfry until the bacon is crisp, about 10 minutes. Cut into bite-size pieces and stir into the soup.

5. Pour the chicken stock into the hot skillet and stir to dissolve any brown flavor bits; add the chicken stock to the soup. Season with sea salt and pepper. Lastly, add the peppercorns.
6. Set the cooker to low heat and cook the soup until the beans are very tender, 6 to 8 hours. Mash about half the beans with a potato masher to thicken the soup before serving.

Yield: 8 Servings
Degree of Difficulty: Moderately Difficult
Preparation Time: 45 minutes
Cooking Time: 8 hours
Total Time: 8 hours and 45 minutes

Recipe Type

Main Dish, Soups

LOADED BAKED POTATO SOUP

We tried making this after ordering a similar dish at a local restaurant and falling in love with it. It's easy to make; I especially enjoy it on a cold winter's day. Here it is for you, my dear.

"Never let the things you want make you forget the things you have."

—Unknown

6 c. whole milk
1/2 c. butter
3/4 c. green onion, chopped
5 medium baked potatoes
2/3 c. all-purpose flour
6 slices bacon, cooked crumbled

1 1/2 c. sour cream
1 garlic clove, minced
1/2 tsp. salt
1/2 tsp. ground black pepper
1 c. sharp cheddar cheese, shredded

Procedure

1. Bake potatoes ahead of time. When cool, peel potatoes and mash coarsely. Discard skins and set potatoes aside.

2. Place flour in a large dutch oven; gradually add milk and whisk until smooth. Cook over medium heat, about 8 minutes, until thickened. Add mashed potatoes, 3/4 cup cheddar cheese, salt, and pepper, stirring until cheese is melted. Remove from heat.

3. Stir in sour cream and half of the onions; cook over low heat for 10 minutes or until thoroughly heated (do not boil). Sprinkle each serving with extra cheese, onion, and bacon.

Yield: 6 Servings
Degree of Difficulty: Easy
Preparation Time: 15 minutes
Cooking Time: 30 minutes
Total Time: 45 minutes

Recipe Type

Main Dish, Soups

MAMA'S LENTIL CHILI

This is a recipe that I used to make quite a bit when you were growing up. I liked the idea of the lentils and the turkey sausage. These ingredients made the chili a little different from what we were used to. You seemed to like it, so I'm including it for you to make in your home now that you're all grown up!

"Speak from the heart and the truth will be shown."

—Jean Paul-Alice

2 Tbs. olive oil
1 medium onion
2 cloves garlic, minced
1 (8-oz.) package Jimmy Dean turkey sausage
1 lb. beef stew meat
1 Tbs. chili powder
2 tsp. red pepper flake

1 tsp. cumin
1 (14.5-oz.) can tomatoes
1 (10-oz.) can Ro-Tel tomatoes
1 (12-oz.) pkg. lentils, rinsed and sorted
8 c. water
1 Tbs. Better Than Bouillon Beef Base
Salt and pepper to taste

Procedure

1. In large dutch oven, heat olive oil on high heat. Add garlic and onion and cook until translucent.
2. Add turkey sausage and stew meat; cook until browned. Add chili powder, red pepper flakes, cumin, tomatoes, Ro-Tel tomatoes, lentils, water, and bouillon.
3. Bring to a boil on high; lower to a simmer for 30 to 40 minutes. Add salt and pepper to taste. Enjoy.

Yield: 10 Servings
Degree of Difficulty: Easy
Preparation Time: 10 minutes
Cooking Time: 45 minutes
Total Time: 55 minutes

Recipe Type

Main Dish, Soups

SEAFOOD GUMBO

Do you remember the Christmas that you wanted to have gumbo for Christmas instead of the traditional fare? This is the recipe that we used, and boy was it good! It made a big potful, and we ate it for a couple of days afterwards. It was a Christmas to remember because of this dish. Thanks for the memories, honey!

> "You are loved more than you will ever know by someone who died to know you."
> —Romans 5:8

1/2 tsp. ground cayenne pepper
1/2 tsp. ground white pepper
1/2 tsp. ground black pepper
1 1/2 tsp. paprika
1/2 tsp. dried thyme
1/2 tsp. dried oregano
1/4 c. oil
6 Tbs. flour
1 bay leaf, crushed
1 tsp. salt
3/4 c. vegetable oil
2 c. celery, chopped
2 c. onion, chopped

2 c. green bell pepper, chopped
1 tsp. garlic, minced
3 Tbs. filé powder
2 tsp. hot pepper sauce
1 1/2 c. tomato sauce
7 c. fish stock
2 c. oysters, shucked
1 c. crabmeat
1 lb. small shrimp, peeled and deveined; reserve shells for stock
4 c. cut okra (fresh or frozen)
4 c. andouille sausage, cut into 1/2-inch cubes

Procedure

1. In large dutch oven, combine oil and flour. Cook over medium heat, stirring constantly until roux has browned to a light chocolate color. Add onion, pepper, celery, and garlic. Sauté for 2 to 3 minutes, stirring constantly.

2. Combine the cayenne, white and black peppers, paprika, thyme, oregano, bay leaf, and salt; set aside.

3. Add filé powder, hot pepper sauce, and the pepper-herb mixture. Cook for 5 minutes, stirring constantly. Add tomato sauce and stir as it reduces over high heat. Add fish stock and bring to a boil. Reduce heat and simmer for 1 hour, stirring occasionally.

4. When ready to serve, add shrimp, oysters, and crabmeat. Cover and wait 5 minutes. Turn off heat and let stand for 10 minutes. Serve with rice, if desired.

Yield: 8 Servings
Degree of Difficulty: Moderately difficult
Preparation Time: 15 minutes
Cooking Time: 1 hour and 15 minutes
Total Time: 1 hour and 30 minutes

Recipe Type

Main Dish, Stew

SPLIT PEA AND HAM SOUP

Grandpa Rich used to love Split Pea and Ham Soup. He would absolutely love this recipe. It is rich and thick and has lots of ham in it. It is delicious, so be sure to try it out quickly, honey!

"Faith is not Believing that God can, it is Knowing that He will."

—Author Unknown

1 lb. dried split peas	1 lb. ham, chopped
1 ham hock	1 tsp. salt
3 Tbs. unsalted butter	3/4 tsp. freshly ground black pepper
1 c. finely chopped yellow onion	1/4 tsp. crushed red pepper flakes
1/2 c. finely chopped celery	8 c. chicken broth
1/2 c. finely chopped carrot	1 bay leaf
2 tsp. minced garlic	2 tsp. fresh thyme

Procedure

1. Place the peas in a large pot or bowl; cover with chicken water by 2 inches and soak 8 hours or overnight. Drain the peas and set aside.

2. Score the ham hock. Place in a pot, cover with water, and bring to a boil. Reduce heat and let simmer for 1 hour. Drain and set aside.

3. In a large pot, melt the butter over medium-high heat. Add the onions and cook, stirring, for 2 minutes. Add the celery and carrots and continue stirring until just soft, about 3 minutes. Add the garlic and cook, stirring, for 30 more seconds. Add the ham hock and chopped ham and cook, stirring, until beginning to brown. Add the drained peas, salt, pepper, and pepper flakes, and cook, stirring for 2 minutes.

4. Add 8 cups of chicken broth, the bay leaf and thyme, and cook, stirring occasionally, until the peas are tender, about 1 hour. (Add more chicken broth as needed, if the soup becomes too thick or dry.) Remove the bay leaf and discard. Adjust the seasoning, to taste, and serve immediately.

Yield: 8 Servings
Degree of Difficulty: Easy
Preparation Time: 8 hours
Cooking Time: 50 minutes
Total Time: 8 hours and 50 minutes

Recipe Type

Main Dish, Soups

YUMMY MINESTRONE

We paired this minestrone with Malena's butter crescents and had a great dinner! It tasted good, and we had leftovers to boot. Craig will love it. You may remember grating parmesan cheese over the top of a big bowl of this soup. It does make a big batch, but you can freeze those if you want. You've got to try this one for sure, honey. The fact that it has red wine in it should pique your interest!

> "There are so many fragile things after all. People break so easily, and so do dreams and hearts."
>
> —Neil Gaiman

3 Tbs. olive oil
3 cloves garlic, minced
2 onions, chopped
2 c. celery, chopped
5 carrots, sliced
2 c. chicken stock
2 c. water
4 c. tomato sauce
1/2 c. red wine (optional)

1 c. canned kidney beans, drained
1 (15-oz.) can green beans
2 c. fresh baby spinach, rinsed
3 zucchini, quartered and sliced
1 Tbs. chopped fresh oregano
2 Tbs. chopped fresh basil
Salt and pepper to taste
1 c. rotini
2 Tbs. grated parmesan cheese for topping

Procedure

1. In a large stock pot over medium-low heat, heat olive oil and sauté garlic for 2 to 3 minutes. Add onion and sauté for 4 to 5 minutes more. Add celery and carrots; sauté for 1 to 2 minutes. Add chicken broth, water, and tomato sauce and bring to boil, stirring frequently. If desired, add red wine at this point. Reduce heat to low and add kidney beans, green beans, spinach leaves, zucchini, oregano, basil, salt, and pepper. Simmer for 30 to 40 minutes —the longer the better.

2. Fill a medium saucepan with water and bring to a boil. Add pasta and cook until tender. Drain water and set aside. Once pasta is cooked, add to stock pot and continue cooking an additional 30 minutes. Ladle soup into bowls and grate fresh parmesan cheese on top.

Yield: 8 Servings
Degree of Difficulty: Easy
Preparation Time: 35 minutes
Cooking Time: 50 minutes
Total Time: 1 hour and 25 minutes

Recipe Type

Main Dish, Soups

9. SWEETS AND DESSERTS

AUNT VICKI'S MELT-IN-YOUR-MOUTH DESSERT

This is a favorite recipe of your Aunt Vicki. It's rich and delicious. She includes tips to make it lower in calories; this allows it to be a favorite of mine! Try making this dessert when you need to wow someone; you'll be the hit of the party!

> "The best and most beautiful things in the world cannot be seen or even touched—they must be felt with the heart.
>
> —Helen Keller

Crust
1 c. flour
1/2 c. butter
1 c. pecans, finely chopped

1st Layer
8 oz. cream cheese, softened
1 c. powdered sugar
1 8-ounce container Cool Whip

2nd layer
1 small box chocolate fudge instant pudding
1 small box cheesecake instant pudding
3 c. milk

3rd Layer
1 8-ounce container Cool Whip
Cream Cheese Frosting
1 1.55-ounce Hershey bar

Procedure

1. Crust: Mix flour, butter, and pecans and press into 9x13-inch pan; bake at 350 degrees F until golden brown, about 10–15 min. Cool completely.

2. First Layer: Blend together cream cheese and powdered sugar. Fold in whipped topping. Add just enough milk, about 1/4 cup, to spread smoothly over crust. Chill completely.

3. Second Layer: Combine chocolate fudge pudding and cheesecake pudding with milk and mix for 2 to 3 minutes until pudding begins to thicken. Spread over first layer and chill completely.

4. Third Layer: Spread Cool Whip Cream Cheese Frosting over second layer. Grate Hershey's bar over top. Chill completely.

5. Notes: To make more diet-friendly, use margarine in place of butter and fat-free or low fat cream cheese in place of the regular version. You can also use Cool Whip Lite in place of the original version and sugar free puddings if you can find them.

Yield: 24 Servings
Degree of Difficulty: Easy
Preparation Time: 30 minutes
Cooking Time: 15 minutes
Inactive Time: 2 hours
Total Time: 2 hours and 45 minutes

Recipe Type

Dessert

CHEWY PUMPKIN BARS

These are the ooey-gooey pumpkin bars that you prefer. Now that it's here, in printed form, you will always know where to find the recipe. Since you said they are so delicious, I am going to try them as well. You have good judgment, my love.

"Nothing in life is to be feared, it is only to be understood."

—Marie Curie

1 yellow cake mix
4 large eggs
1 c. unsalted butter, melted and divided
1 (8-oz.) package cream cheese, softened
1 (15-oz.) can pumpkin

1 (16-oz.) package powdered sugar
1 tsp. cinnamon
1 tsp. nutmeg
1 tsp. vanilla extract

Procedure

1. Preheat oven to 350 degrees F.
2. In medium mixing bowl, combine cake mix, 1 large egg, and 1/2 cup melted butter. Press into a greased 9x13-inch pan. Set aside.
3. In medium mixing bowl, combine 3 large eggs and cream cheese. Once well-combined and fluffy, add pumpkin puree; mix well. Add powdered sugar, cinnamon, nutmeg, and vanilla. Combine well. Add remaining 1/2 cup melted butter and mix until all ingredients are well-combined. Pour wet ingredients over crust.
4. Bake 40–50 minutes or until knife inserted in center comes out clean. Cool completely before cutting into bars.

Yield: 24 Servings
Degree of Difficulty: Easy
Oven Temperature: 350°F
Preparation Time: 15 minutes
Cooking Time: 40 minutes
Total Time: 55 minutes

Recipe Type

Cakes, Pastries, and Desserts

CHOCOLATE AND ALMOND BISCOTTI

I love to make biscotti, especially at Christmastime. These Italian cookies are great for dunking in coffee. I always make three or four different kinds, and this is one flavor. There isn't a lot of sugar in them, so they are not too sweet. They are double-baked, and I think that is why they're so hard and crunchy. You always seemed to like them, so I am including the recipe in your cookbook, sweetheart.

"When a woman becomes her own best friend, things become easier."

—Unknown

1 1/2 c. blanched whole almonds
2 c. all-purpose flour
1 tsp. baking soda
1/2 tsp. baking powder
1/2 tsp. salt
1 c. granulated sugar

1 1/2 c. semisweet chocolate chips
2 large eggs
2 egg whites
1 tsp. vanilla extract
2 Tbs. whiskey

Procedure

1. Preheat oven to 350 degrees F.
2. Toast the almonds in a shallow pan for 12 to 15 minutes, shaking the pan a few times, until almonds are lightly browned. Set aside to cool.
3. Increase oven temperature to 375 degrees F.
4. Line 2 or 3 cookie sheets with parchment paper. In a large bowl, stir together the flour, baking soda, baking powder, salt, and sugar. Place 1/2 cup of dry ingredients into the bowl of a food processor. Add about a half cup of the toasted almonds and process for about 30 seconds. Return the mixture to the bowl of dry ingredients and stir in the remaining almonds and chocolate chips.
5. In a large measuring cup, beat the eggs, egg whites, vanilla, and whiskey together with a whisk. Stir this mixture into the dry ingredients until moistened. Wet your hands and divide the dough into four portions. Keeping hands wet, form each quarter into strips about 9 inches long, 2 inches wide, and 1/2 inch high. Round the ends. Place two strips crosswise on each of the cookie sheets. Bake for 25 minutes. If baking more than one sheet at a time, reverse the sheets top to bottom halfway through cooking time. Using a metal spatula, remove the slabs from cookie sheets and let cool for 20 minutes on cutting board.
6. Reduce oven temperature to 275 degrees F. With a serrated knife, carefully cut at an angle into slices, about 1/2-inch wide. Place the slices, cut-side down, onto cookie sheets. Bake 25 to 30 minutes, until crispy and lightly toasted. Turn oven off and open the oven door, allowing the biscotti to cool in the oven. When cool, store in an airtight container.

Yield: 72 Servings
Degree of Difficulty: Moderately Difficult
Preparation Time: 30 minutes
Cooking Time: 45 minutes
Total Time: 1 hour and 15 minutes

Recipe Type

Cookies

COCONUT LIME BARS

I first made this recipe when you were a young teen, going to Skutt Catholic High School. You would ask me to make these while you were entertaining your girlfriends. Besides the fact that these bars are scrumptious, they're also super easy and quick to make. I hope this recipe brings back fond memories.

> "Beautiful in my opinion has nothing to do with looks. It's how you are as a person and how you make others feel about themselves."
>
> —Unknown

Crust
8 Tbs. cold butter (cut in 1/2-tsp. pieces)
1/2 c. brown sugar
1/3 c. granulated sugar
1 large egg
3/4 c. macadamia nuts, chopped
1 c. all-purpose flour
1/2 tsp. salt
1/4 c. confectioner's sugar
2 Tbs. freshly grated lime zest

Filling
4 large eggs
1 c. sugar
1/3 c. all-purpose flour
1/2 c. fresh lime juice, plus 2 Tbs. lime juice
1 Tbs. freshly grated lime zest
Garnish
1/3 c. sweetened flaked coconut

Procedure

1. Preheat oven to 375 degrees F.
2. Butter a 9-inch square baking pan and line with parchment paper, leaving a 2-inch overhang on two sides.
3. Use fingertips to blend together butter, brown sugar, and 1/3 cup granulated sugar until mixture resembles coarse meal.
4. Add 1 egg; whisk until smooth. Stir in 1 cup flour, salt, nuts, and lime zest.
5. Pat mixture into prepared pan and bake in middle of oven for 15 to 18 minutes or until golden brown.
6. For filling: Whisk together eggs, sugar, flour, fresh lime juice, and lime zest until combined well; stir in flour, and zest.
7. Pour filling mixture over crust and bake in middle of oven for 20 minutes.
8. Top custard with coconut garnish and bake 5 to 10 minutes longer, just until set.
9. Set on rack and cool 1 hour.
10. Cut into 2-inch squares.

Yield: 16 Servings
Degree of Difficulty: Easy
Oven Temperature: 325°F
Preparation Time: 10 minutes
Inactive Time: 50 minutes
Total Time: 1 hour

Recipe Type

Cookies and Bars, Dessert

DADDY'S HOMEMADE ICE CREAM

This is Daddy's recipe, and I thought you would like to have it in your collection. He made it all the time, and you loved eating it when you were growing up. Now you can make it for your family, sweetheart!

> "At the center of your being, you have the answer; you know who you are and you know what you want."
>
> —Lau Tzu

6 large eggs
1 1/2 c. sugar
3/4 tsp. salt

2 c. table cream
6 c. whole milk
2–3 Tbs. vanilla extract

Procedure

1. In large mixing bowl, combine eggs, sugar, and salt; mix well. Add remaining ingredients and mix until frothy. Pour into the canister of ice-cream maker. Freeze until solid. Eat immediately or transfer to covered container and freeze for up to 8 hours.

Yield: 12 Servings (2 qt.)
Degree of Difficulty: Easy

Preparation Time: 15 minutes
Cooking Time: 1 hour
Total Time: 1 hour and 15 minutes

Recipe Type

Dessert

GRANDMA JOYCE'S OVEN CARAMEL CORN

Grandma Joyce's famous caramel corn is another Christmas favorite. She makes it every year, and everybody clamors for it. I asked her for the recipe, and she happily obliged. I have made followed the recipe before, and it is very good. It is simple to prepare, and it makes a big batch. One helpful hint I will add: buy popcorn from the store, and then caramelize it at home. This prevents you from the tedious task of sorting through the corn for unpopped kernels. Doing this also cuts down on the time the recipe takes. It is a delicious recipe either way. Make a batch and keep it in a bowl that can be resealed to keep it fresh. I hope you like it, honey.

"Giving opens the way for receiving."
—Florence Scovel Shinn

8 quarts popped corn
2 c. brown sugar
1 c. margarine
1 tsp. salt

1/2 c. white corn syrup
1 tsp. vanilla extract
1/2 tsp. baking soda

Procedure

1. Preheat oven to 250 degrees F.
2. Combine brown sugar, margarine, salt, corn syrup, and vanilla. Boil for 5 minutes, stirring occasionally. Remove from the heat and add baking soda. Pour over popped corn, mixing well. Put in large flat pan and place in preheated oven for 50 to 60 minutes, stirring 3 or 4 times. Once cooled, it keeps indefinitely in an airtight container. Peanuts may be added if desired.

Yield: 12 Servings
Degree of Difficulty: Easy
Oven Temperature: 250°F
Preparation Time: 15 minutes
Cooking Time: 1 hour
Total Time: 1 hour and 15 minutes

Recipe Type

Snack

GRANDMA WILSON'S RED VELVET CAKE

This recipe came from Curt's mother, and it has been handed down through three generations now. The frosting is not typical for a red velvet cake, as it has a thinner consistency and looks somewhat curdled. However, do not let its appearance fool you. It is absolutely delicious and tastes just as good as any red velvet cake. This cake recipe is a keeper. The entire bottle of red food coloring listed in the ingredients is not a typo. Try this recipe when you can, honey!

> "It takes courage to grow up and turn out to be who you really are."
>
> —e. e. cummings

1/2 c. plus 1 Tbs. shortening
2 large eggs
1 1/2 c. granulated sugar
1 (1-oz.) bottle red food coloring
1 tsp. vanilla extract
2 tsp. cocoa powder
1 tsp. salt
1 c. buttermilk
2 1/2 c. cake flour

1 tsp. baking soda
1 tsp. vinegar
Frosting
4 1/2 Tbs. all-purpose flour
1 1/2 c. milk
1 1/2 c. butter, softened
1 1/2 c. granulated sugar
1 1/2 tsp. vanilla extract

Procedure

1. Preheat oven to 350 degrees F. Grease and flour two 9-inch round baking pans. Set aside.
2. In large mixing bowl, cream shortening and sugar until well-blended. Add eggs one at a time; blend well.
3. Make a paste of food coloring and cocoa powder. Add to mixture and blend well. Add buttermilk and salt.
4. Add cake flour, baking soda, vinegar, and vanilla extract. Blend well.
5. Divide cake batter between prepared pans. Bake for 30 minutes or until toothpick inserted in center comes out clean.
6. Invert cakes onto racks to cool. Once cool, cut each layer in half horizontally so that you have 4 layers of equal size.
7. To make frosting, combine milk and flour in small saucepan and cook until thin; allow to cool.
8. In medium bowl, cream butter and sugar until fluffy. Add cooled milk mixture and mix well. Add vanilla extract.
9. Put first layer of cake on cake plate and ice with a quarter of frosting. Put second cake layer on top and continue until all layers are frosted. Enjoy!

Yield: 12 Servings
Degree of Difficulty: Moderately Difficult
Oven Temperature: 350°F
Preparation Time: 25 minutes
Cooking Time: 30 minutes
Total Time: 55 minutes

Recipe Type

Cakes, Pastries, and Desserts

KRISPY CARAMEL BARS

These are a step up from traditional Rice Krispies Treats. How could you go wrong with the mix of sweet and salty these bars provide? Try this recipe, and you'll never go back to the old version.

> "Face your deficiencies and acknowledge them; but do not let them master you. Let them teach you patience, sweetness, insight."
>
> —Helen Keller

6 c. Rice Krispies
1/2 c. butter
1/2 can brown sugar
1/4 c. heavy cream

1 Tbs. light corn syrup
2 tsp. sea salt, plus more for sprinkling
1 (10-oz.) bag miniature marshmallows

Procedure

1. Spray 8-inch square baking dish. Set aside.
2. Measure 6 c. Rice Krispies cereal into large heatproof bowl; set aside.
3. In a medium saucepan over medium heat, melt 1/2 cup butter. Once melted, add brown sugar, cream, and corn syrup. Continue cooking until thick and syrupy, about 7or 8 minutes. Stir in the salt.
4. Turn off heat and stir in miniature marshmallows. Stir until completely melted.
5. Pour mixture over Rice Krispies and stir until completely coated.
6. Pour into prepared pan and press with back of spoon or spatula sprayed with cooking spray.
7. Sprinkle lightly with additional sea salt.
8. Cut when cool.

Yield: 24 Servings
Degree of Difficulty: Easy
Preparation Time: 20 minutes
Cooking Time: 10 minutes

Recipe Type

Dessert, Snack

MAMA'S BEST CHOCOLATE CHIP COOKIES

I made these cookies regularly while you were growing up, and they were your favorites. I also got more compliments on them than with any other cookie. The oats keep the cookies from getting too dry. I also like to add chopped macadamia nuts to the recipe sometimes to have some variety. So here's a "secret recipe" from my kitchen to yours, sweetie pie.

"Life is better when you're laughing!"
—Unknown

1 1/2 c. all-purpose flour
1 tsp. salt
1 tsp. baking soda
1 c. shortening
1 c. packed brown sugar
1/2 c. granulated sugar

1 tsp. vanilla extract
2 large eggs
2 c. rolled oats
2 c. semisweet chocolate chips
1 c. chopped macadamia nuts (optional)

Procedure

1. Preheat oven to 350 degrees F.
2. Line baking sheets with parchment paper. Combine flour, salt, and baking soda on waxed paper. Beat together shortening, sugars, and vanilla in large bowl with electric mixer until creamy. Add eggs and beat until light and fluffy. Gradually beat in flour mixture. Stir in rolled oats and then chocolate chips. Drop batter by rounded teaspoonfuls onto baking sheets. Bake for 8 to 10 minutes or until golden. Cool cookies on sheets for 2 minutes. Remove to wire racks to cool completely.

Yield: 24 Servings (4 dozen cookies)
Degree of Difficulty: Easy
Oven Temperature: 350°F
Preparation Time: 20 minutes
Cooking Time: 10 minutes

Recipe Type

Cookies

MAMA'S FLAKY PIE CRUST

This is my recipe for pie crust. You always liked it because it was a little sweet, which makes it good for sweet pies. I don't use this crust for savory recipes, such as pot pies or quiches, because it is so sweet. It's an easy recipe to make, especially because I converted it to be made in a food processor, like Grandpa taught me. But you can make it by hand if you don't have a food processor. The trick is to make sure all the ingredients are ice-cold before you start to prepare the recipe. This will ensure a perfect crust, tender and flaky. I hope you have good luck with this recipe.

"What if you wake up today with only the things you thanked God for yesterday?"
—Unknown

2 1/2 c. all-purpose flour
1/4 tsp. salt
3 Tbs. sugar
1/4 c. vegetable shortening, cold

12 Tbs. butter, cold and cubed
1/4 to 1/2 c. ice water
3 Tbs. butter, diced

Procedure

1. In food processor, sift together the flour, salt, and sugar. Add the shortening, in small amounts, directly into the flour. Add the cold butter cubes through the food processor chute while the appliance is running. To keep the butter from getting too soft, pulse the food processor quickly until the mixture is crumbly, like very coarse cornmeal. Continue pulsing and add the ice water a little at a time until the mixture comes together, forming dough.

2. Bring the dough together into a ball and stop working it; otherwise, the dough will get overworked and tough. Divide the dough in half and flatten it slightly to form disk shapes. Wrap each disk in plastic and chill in the refrigerator for about 30 minutes.

3. Preheat oven to 450 degrees F. Roll out dough as needed for pies. Makes two crusts.

Yield: 12 Servings
Degree of Difficulty: Moderately Difficult
Preparation Time: 10 minutes
Inactive Time: 30 minutes
Total Time: 40 minutes

Recipe Type

Dessert

MANGO ICE CREAM

I just love homemade ice cream the day that it's made. It seems that if you go to eat it after that, it gets hard and, well, icy. When I made this recipe for the first time, I was pleased with the flavor and consistency, but the day after, I was ecstatic! The ice cream was firm yet still soft enough to easily eat without a chisel. We have since made this recipe with strawberries and blackberries; however, I recommend straining the blackberry mixture before pouring it into the ice-cream machine. You can try making it with just about any fruit; the sky's the limit. This recipe gets five stars on my list. If you try it, you'll see what I mean. Enjoy!

> "We make a living by what we get, we make a life by what we give."
> —Sir Winston Churchill

1 (16-oz.) pkg. frozen mangoes
1 1/2 c. heavy cream, divided
3/4 c. sugar

3 large egg yolks
3 Tbs. corn syrup

Procedure

1. Thaw mangoes and place into the container of a blender or food processor and puree until smooth. Pour into a large bowl and set aside.

2. Heat 1 1/4 cups of the cream in a saucepan over medium heat until bubbles appear at the edge of the pan. In a large bowl, whisk together the sugar, egg yolks, remaining 1/4 cup of cream, and corn syrup. Gradually pour the hot cream into the egg yolk mixture, whisking constantly. Return the mixture to the saucepan and heat until mixture is thick enough to coat the back of a metal spoon, about 5 minutes. Do not allow it to boil. Mix and then refrigerate until chilled.

3. Fill an ice-cream maker with the mixture and freeze according to the manufacturer's instructions.

4. Note: You may substitute any fruit for the mangoes.

Yield: 6 Servings
Degree of Difficulty: Easy
Preparation Time: 10 minutes
Cooking Time: 45 minutes
Total Time: 55 minutes

Recipe Type

Dessert

RUSTIC APPLE TART

I always laugh a little under my breath when I mention the subject of making a pie to you, especially if we're talking face-to-face. You seem to have the fear of God in your eyes. Seriously, honey, making a piecrust isn't that difficult, although I admit that I had a hard time making my first one. This recipe is a good dish because you can mess up the crust, and nobody has to know about it. You can patch it as many times as you wish. And it's delicious as well! Try this one on company sometime, and you'll really impress them!

"I love you to the moon and back!"
—Mom

Pastry
1 1/4 c. all purpose-flour
1 stick very cold unsalted butter, cut into small pieces
3 Tbs. ice water
2 tsp. lemon peel
1 tsp. lemon juice

Filling
4 large golden delicious or granny smith apples (about 1 1/2 pounds), peeled
1/4 c. sugar
1/2 tsp. ground nutmeg
2 Tbs. butter
Confectioner's sugar (optional)

Procedure

1. To make the pastry in food processor: Process flour and butter until coarse crumbs form. With the motor running, add the water, lemon peel, and juice through the feed tube and process until the dough leaves the sides of the bowl. Gather the dough into a ball, flatten, wrap in waxed paper, and refrigerate for 30 minutes or until firm enough to roll out.

2. To make the filling: Cut each apple in half from top to bottom. Remove the core and cut out stem and bud ends. Turn the halves cut-side down and thinly slice.

3. Preheat the oven to 425 degrees F.

4. On a lightly floured surface, roll the dough into a 13-inch round. (The edges can be uneven.) Transfer to an ungreased cookie sheet. Leaving a 2-inch border, arrange the apple slices in concentric circles, starting at the outside. In a small cup, mix the sugar and nutmeg. Sprinkle the mixture over the apples and then dot with the remaining butter. Fold the edges of the pastry over the apples. Bake for 15 minutes. Reduce the oven to 375 degrees F and bake until the apples are tender and pastry is golden, about 35 minutes more. Slide the tart onto a wire rack to cool. Before serving, dust with confectioners' sugar if desired.

Yield: 8 Servings
Degree of Difficulty: Moderately Difficult
Oven Temperature: 375°F
Preparation Time: 20 minutes
Cooking Time: 50 minutes
Total Time: 1 hour and 10 minutes

Recipe Type

Cakes, Pastries, and Desserts

SINFUL PUMPKIN BARS

You said you made the Chewy Pumpkin Bars this year, in 2012, so I thought I would also give you my recipe for the cake-like variety. These are absolutely sinful, thanks to the cream cheese icing. The recipe makes a large panful of bars, and they are rich, so I usually cut about 36 pieces, but you can make them bigger if you wish. Try them if you like, but don't tell me I didn't warn you—they are addictive!

"Do small things with great love."
—Unknown

Bars
4 large eggs
1 2/3 c. granulated sugar
1 c. vegetable oil
1 (15-oz.) can pumpkin puree
2 c. sifted all-purpose flour
2 tsp. baking powder
2 tsp. ground cinnamon

1 tsp. salt
1 tsp. baking soda
Icing
1 (8-oz.) pkg. cream cheese, softened
1/2 c. butter, softened
2 c. sifted confectioners' sugar
1 tsp. vanilla extract

Procedure

1. Preheat the oven to 350 degrees F.
2. Using an electric mixer at medium speed, combine the eggs, sugar, oil, and pumpkin puree until light and fluffy. Stir together the flour, baking powder, cinnamon, salt, and baking soda. Add the dry ingredients to the pumpkin mixture and beat at low speed until thoroughly combined and the batter is smooth. Spread the batter into a greased 13x10-inch baking pan. Bake for 30 minutes. Let cool completely before frosting. Cut into bars.
3. To make the icing: Combine the cream cheese and butter in a medium bowl with an electric mixer until smooth and fluffy. Add the sugar and mix at low speed until combined. Stir in vanilla and mix again. Spread on cooled pumpkin bars.

Yield: 36 Servings
Degree of Difficulty: Easy
Oven Temperature: 350°F
Preparation Time: 15 minutes
Cooking Time: 30 minutes
Total Time: 45 minutes

Recipe Type

Cakes, Pastries, and Desserts

GLOSSARY

GLOSSARY OF COOKING TERMINOLOGY

Just like any other activity, cooking has its own vocabulary. This glossary isn't a complete list, but it will help you learn some of the most common terms.

1. Al dente: Description for pasta that is cooked until tender but firm to the bite.
2. Bake: To cook food in an oven with dry heat. Bake food uncovered for a dry, crisp top (e.g., breads, cakes, cookies, and chicken) or covered to retain moistness (e.g., vegetables, casseroles, and stews).
3. Baste: Spoon liquid over food (e.g., baste pan juices over turkey) during cooking to keep it moist.
4. Batter: An uncooked mixture of flour, eggs, liquid, and other ingredients. Batter is thin enough to be spooned or poured (e.g., muffins or pancakes).
5. Blanch: Plunge food into boiling water for a brief time to preserve color, texture, and nutritional value or to remove the skin (e.g., with vegetables, fruits, and nuts).
6. Boil: Heat liquid until bubbles rise continuously and break on the surface and steam is given off. In a rolling boil, the bubbles form rapidly and the surface appears to roll.
7. Bread: Coat a food (e.g., fish, meat, or vegetables) by dipping into a liquid (such as beaten egg or milk) and then into bread crumbs, cracker crumbs, or cornmeal before frying or baking. *See also* Coat.
8. Broil: Cook directly under a red-hot heating unit.
9. Brown: Cook quickly over high heat, causing the surface of the food to turn brown.
10. Caramelize: Melt sugar slowly over low heat until it becomes a golden-brown caramel-flavored syrup. Or sprinkle granulated, powdered, or brown sugar on top of a food and then place it under a broiler until the sugar is melted and caramelized.
11. Chill: Place food in the refrigerator until it's thoroughly cold.
12. Chop: Cut food into coarse or fine irregular-shaped pieces, using a knife, food chopper, blender, or food processor.
13. Coat: Cover food evenly with crumbs or sauce. *See also* Bread.
14. Cool: Allow hot food to stand at room temperature until it reaches a desired temperature. Placing hot food on a wire rack will help it cool more quickly. Occasional stirring will help a mixture cool more quickly and evenly.
15. Core: Remove the center of a fruit (e.g., apple, pear, or pineapple). Some cores contain small seeds (apple or pear); others are woody (pineapple).
16. Cover: Place a cover, a lid, plastic wrap, or aluminum foil over a container of food.
17. Crisp-tender: Description of doneness for vegetables cooked so that they retain some of their crisp texture.
18. Crush: Press into very fine particles; for example, crushing a clove of garlic with a chef's knife or garlic press.
19. Cube: Cut food into squares 1/2 inch or larger, using a knife.

20. Cut up: Cut food into small, irregular pieces, using kitchen scissors or a knife. Or cut a large food into smaller pieces (e.g., with broiler-fryer chickens).

21. Dash: Less than 1/8 teaspoon of an ingredient.

22. Deep fry or french fry: Cook in hot fat that's deep enough to float the food. *See also* Fry, Panbroil, Panfry, and Sauté.

23. Deglaze: After panfrying a food, remove excess fat from the skillet and then add a small amount of liquid (e.g., broth, water, or wine) and stir to loosen browned bits of food. This mixture is used as a base for sauce.

24. Dice: Cut food into squares smaller than 1/2 inch, using a knife.

25. Dissolve: Stir a dry ingredient (e.g., flavored gelatin, yeast, or sugar) into a liquid ingredient (e.g., boiling water, hot water, or tea) until the dry ingredient dissolves.

26. Dip: Moisten or coat a food by submerging it, covering all sides.

27. Dough: A stiff but pliable mixture of flour, liquid, and other ingredients (often including a type of leavening). Dough can be dropped from a spoon (cookies), rolled (pie crust), or kneaded (bread).

28. Drain: Pour off liquid by putting the food into a strainer or colander that has been set in the sink. If draining fat from meat, place the strainer in a disposable container. If you're saving the liquid, place the strainer in a bowl or other container.

29. Drizzle: Pour topping in thin lines from a spoon or liquid measuring cup in an uneven pattern over food (e.g., for glaze over cake or cookies).

30. Dust: Sprinkle lightly with flour, granulated sugar, powdered sugar, or baking cocoa (e.g., dusting coffee cake with powdered sugar).

31. Flake: Break lightly into small pieces, using a fork (e.g., cooked fish).

32. Flute: Pinching pastry with your fingers to make a finished, decorative edge.

33. Fry: Cook in hot fat over moderate or high heat. *See also* Deep fry, Panbroil, Panfry, Sauté.

34. Garnish: Decorate a dish with small amounts of other foods that have a distinctive color or texture (e.g., parsley, fresh berries, or chocolate curls).

35. Glaze: Brush, spread, or drizzle an ingredient (such as meat stock, jam, or melted chocolate) on hot or cold food to give it a glossy appearance or hard finish.

36. Grate: Rub a hard-textured food (e.g., chocolate, citrus peel, or parmesan cheese) against the small, rough, sharp-edged holes of a grater to reduce it to tiny particles. When grating citrus peel, be sure to grate only the outer skin, not the bitter white inner membrane.

37. Grease: Rub the bottom and sides of a pan with shortening, using pastry brush, waxed paper, or paper towel. Or spray pan with cooking spray. Grease pans to prevent food from sticking during baking (e.g., muffins and some casseroles). Don't use butter or margarine for greasing unless specified in a recipe; they usually contain salt that may cause hot foods to stick.

38. Grease and flour: After greasing a pan with shortening, sprinkle it with small amount of flour and shake the pan to distribute it evenly. Then, turn the pan upside down and tap the bottom to remove excess flour. Do this to prevent sticking during baking.

39. Grill: Cooking outdoors on an outdoors cooking unit, either using charcoal briquettes or gas.
40. Heat oven: Turn the oven control(s) to the desired temperature, allowing the oven to heat thoroughly before adding food. Preheating takes about 10 minutes for most ovens.
41. Hull: Remove the stem and leaves with a knife or huller (e.g., strawberries).
42. Husk: Remove the leaves and outer shell (e.g., corn on the cob).
43. Julienne: Cut into thin, match-like strips with a knife or food processor (e.g., fruits, vegetables, and meats).
44. Knead: Work dough on a floured surface into a smooth, elastic mass, using your hands or an electric mixer with a dough hook. Kneading develops the gluten in flour, giving it an even texture and a smooth, rounded top.
45. Marinate: Let food stand in a marinade—a savory, acidic liquid—in a glass or plastic container for several hours to add flavor or to tenderize. Always refrigerate marinating foods.
46. Melt: Turn a solid (e.g., chocolate or butter) into liquid by heating.
47. Microwave: Cook, reheat, or thaw food in a microwave oven.
48. Mince: Cut food into very fine pieces—smaller than chopped, but bigger than crushed—with a knife.
49. Mix: Combine ingredients evenly, using any method.
50. Panbroil: Cook meat or other food quickly in an ungreased or lightly greased skillet.
51. Panfry: Fry meat or other food in a skillet, using varying amounts of fat and usually pouring off the fat during cooking. *See also* Deep fry, Fry, Panbroil, and Sauté.
52. Peel: Cut off the outer covering with a knife or vegetable peeler (apples or potatoes). Also, strip off the outer covering with your fingers (bananas or oranges).
53. Poach: Cook in simmering liquid just below the boiling point (e.g., eggs or fish).
54. Pound: Flatten boneless cuts of chicken and meat, using a meat mallet or the flat side of a meat pounder, until they're a uniform thickness.
55. Puree: Blend food until it's smooth, using a blender or food processor.
56. Reduce: Boil liquid, uncovered, to evaporate some liquid and intensify the flavor of the remaining liquid.
57. Reduce heat: Lower the heat on the stovetop so that a mixture continues to cook slowly and evenly without scorching.
58. Refrigerate: Place food in the refrigerator to chill or store it.
59. Roast: Cook meat, uncovered, on rack in a shallow pan in the oven without adding liquid.
60. Roll: Flatten dough into a thin, even layer, using a rolling pin (e.g., cookies or pie crust).
61. Roll up: Roll a flat food that has been spread with a filling—or with the filling placed at one end—beginning at one end until it is tube-shaped (e.g., jelly roll or enchilada).
62. Sauté: Cook over medium-high heat in a small amount of fat, using a frequent tossing or turning motion. *See also* Deep fry, Fry, Panbroil, Panfry.

63. Scald: Heat liquid to just below the boiling point and you see tiny bubbles forming at the edge. A thin skin will form on the top of scalded milk.

64. Score: Lightly cut the surface of a food about 1/4 inch deep, using a knife. Scoring helps cooking and flavoring; it may also be used for the sake of appearance (e.g., meat or yeast bread).

65. Sear: Brown meat quickly over high heat.

66. Season: Add flavor with salt, pepper, herbs, spices, or seasoning mixes.

67. Shred: Cut into long, thin pieces using the round, smooth holes of shredder, a knife, or a food processor.

68. Simmer: Cook in liquid on the stovetop just below the boiling point while bubbles rise slowly and break just below the surface. Simmering is usually done after reducing heat from a boil.

69. Skim: Remove the top layer of fat or foam floating on top of a soup or broth, using a spoon, ladle, or skimmer (a flat utensil with holes in it).

70. Slice: Cut into flat pieces about the same size (e.g., bread or meat).

71. Snip: Cut into very small pieces with kitchen scissors.

72. Soft Peaks: Egg whites or whipping cream beaten until the moist, glossy peaks are rounded or curl when you lift the beaters from the bowl. *See also* Stiff Peaks.

73. Soften: Let cold food stand at room temperature, or heat in microwave at low power setting, until no longer hard (e.g., butter, margarine, or cream cheese).

74. Steam: Cook food by placing it on a rack or in a special steamer basket over a small amount of boiling water in a covered pan.

75. Stew: Cook slowly in a small amount of liquid for a long time (e.g., stewed fruit or beef stew).

76. Stiff Peaks: Egg whites or whipping cream beaten until moist, glossy peaks stand up straight when you lift the beaters from the bowl. *See also* Soft Peaks.

77. Stir-fry: A Chinese method of quickly cooking similar-sized pieces of food in a small amount of hot oil over high heat, lifting and stirring constantly with a turner or large spoon.

78. Strain: Pour a mixture or a liquid through a fine sieve or strainer to remove larger particles.

79. Tear: Break into pieces with your fingers.

80. Toast: Brown lightly in a toaster, oven, broiler, or skillet (e.g., bread, coconut, or nuts).

81. Toss: Mix ingredients lightly with a lifting motion (e.g., salads or pasta with sauce).

82. Whip: Beat ingredients to add air and increase volume until light and fluffy (e.g., cream or egg whites).

83. Zest: The outside colored layer of citrus fruit (oranges or lemons) that contains aromatic oils and flavor. Also, removing the outside layer of citrus fruit in fine strips, using a knife, citrus zester, or vegetable peeler.

INDEX

A

Apple Jicama Coleslaw 65
Aunt Vicki's Melt-In-Your-Mouth Dessert 105

B

Barbecue Brisket 51
Beanless Bean Dip 3
Beef and Noodles 52
Beef Barley Soup 93
Beef Rouladen 53
Beef Wellington 54
Beginner's Basic Sourdough Starter 25
Bloody Mary 15
Blueberry Surprise Muffins 26
Blue Cheese Dressing 73
Breakfast Crepes with Berries 39
Buffalo Wings 4
Butter Crescents 27

C

Calico Baked Beans 81
Cauliflower Mac-and-Cheese Casserole 82
Cherry Breakfast Scones 28
Chewy Pumpkin Bars 106
Chicken Tortilla Soup 94
Chocolate and Almond Biscotti 107
Cinnabon Clone 29
Classic Creamed Spinach 83
Coconut Lime Bars 108
Corn and Oyster Casserole 84
Cream Cheese Banana Bread 30
Creamed Corn Like No Other 85
Creamy Hot Cocoa 16
Crispy Garlic Parmesan Croutons 67
Curt's Fruit Salad 68
Curt's Stuffed Mushrooms 5

D

Daddy's Corned Beef and Cabbage 55
Daddy's Homemade Ice Cream 109
Daddy's Oyster Soup 95
Delicious Dill Potato Salad 86
Delicious Fruit Dip 6
Dill Dip 7

E

Easy Overnight Caramel Pecan Rolls 40
Egg Drop Soup 96
Eggs Benedict 41

G

German Apple Pancake 42
Glossary of Cooking Terminology 121
Goulash 56
Grandma Joyce's Oven Caramel Corn 110
Grandma Wilson's Red Velvet Cake 111
Greek Vinaigrette Salad Dressing 69

H

Ham and Bean Soup 97
Hash Brown Casserole 87
Healthy Swiss Muesli 43
Holiday Cranberry Nut Bread 31
Holiday Eggnog 17
Homemade Kaluha 18
Hot Apple Cider 19
Hot German Potato Salad 70

K

Krispy Caramel Bars 112

L

Loaded Baked Potato Soup 98
Long Island Iced Tea 20

M

Mama's Beef Stroganoff 57
Mama's Best Chocolate Chip Cookies 113
Mama's Buckwheat Pancakes 44
Mama's Flaky Pie Crust 114
Mama's Fresh Garden Salsa 8
Mama's Garlic House Dressing 71
Mama's Great Guacamole 9
Mama's Lentil Chili 99
Mama's Sweet Potato Soufflé 88
Mango Ice Cream 115
Margarita Recipe 21

O

Omelet Supreme 45

P

Party Sangria 22
Pâté 10
Pioneer Woman's Prime Rib with Rosemary Salt Crust 58
Pumpernickel Rye Bread 32

R

Ramen Broccoli Cole Slaw (Wedding Salad) 72
Red Lobster Cheddar Bay Biscuits Copycat 33
Restaurant-Style Fried Rice 89
Rustic Apple Tart 116

S

Seafood Gumbo 100
Seafood Pasta Salad 74
Simple Simon Salmon 59
Sinful Pumpkin Bars 117
Sour Cream Coffee Cake 46
Sourdough Pancakes 47
Spicy Cornbread 34
Spinach Dip 11
Split Pea and Ham Soup 101
Sprouted Whole Wheat Health Bread 35
Strawberry-Cream Cheese Stuffed French Toast 48
Strawberry Pretzel Salad 75
Sugar-Free Cranberry Relish 66
Sweet Baby Salmon 60
Sweet Orange Tilapia 61

T

Taco Salad 76
Thousand Island Dressing 77
Twice Baked Potatoes 90

Y

Yummy Minestrone 102
Yum Yums 62

Z

Zesty Cocktail Sauce (for Shrimp Cocktail) 12
Zucchini Bread 36